THE ELEMENTS OF CREATION MYTH

The Mighty Forces of Nature

Charlie Dean Jr.

iUniverse, Inc.
New York   Bloomington

THE ELEMENTS OF CREATION MYTH
THE MIGHTY FORCES of NATURE

iUniverse books may be ordered through booksellers or by contacting:

iUniverse
1663 Liberty Drive
Bloomington, IN 47403
www.iuniverse.com
1-800-Authors (1-800-288-4677)

ISBN: 978-1-4502-4197-7 (pbk)
ISBN: 978-1-4502-4198-4 (ebk)

Printed in the United States of America

iUniverse rev. date: 8/19/2010

This writing is about the son of a truck driver that had been given a classroom assignment to ask his family members about their knowledge of creation. His father later wrote a myth titled, "SONNY BABE AIN'T NO MONKEY," which stated that it took not one but eight spirits to create the universe and over time the son could not apprehend the father's myth, causing the father to take a week of his upcoming two weeks vacation to explain his myth to the son.

The father decided to ask his family members permission to allow one week of his upcoming two weeks vacation to spend alone with his son to thoroughly explain his myth. They readily agreed, as the vacation would be spent at the family's farm located in the Mississippi Delta.

After a few more weeks of delivering goods, the father's vacation time had arrived, and the father was up early loading supplies and goodies for the weeks ahead. Later the father joined the other family members around the breakfast table with the son, Sonny Babe being the center of attention, because they were hoping that this will be his beginning of a clearer understanding about the duties of the eight spirits of the father's myth.

"This trip with the son brought back some of the father's childhood memories, as a child about eight years of age the father can remember walking with his father seven miles one way to pick up a writing board for his father's Sunday school class. The folks in the Mississippi Delta call the writing board a blackboard, because the writing board was black with white chalk used for writing instructions for the schools and churches. The father can recall his father saying that he was going to walk seven miles into town and as a child he was ask, if he thought that he could walk seven miles one way and seven miles back. Naturally the son said yes and his father said o. k. and off they went.

"Being a child with a chance to be alone with dad was exciting and the journey was long but the father made it."

"The father can also remember going hunting one night with his father, which seem real exciting and at night seem even more fun he thought, however, before the night was through, night hunting became a nightmare for this little country boy after his father and him spent the night in the woods going in circles until day break. Finally after day break his father became oriented and they returned home. From that time onward the father as a child never wanted to go night hunting again. The father told this little story to say how exciting it must be for the son, Sonny Babe, to have some time alone with his father."

When the meal came to an end the father and son were given hugs and kisses as they were about to begin their trip toward the family's farm located in the Mississippi Delta. Once the trip was underway, a few miles of travel the son was fast asleep and in an uncomfortable position, the father stopped at the first rest stop and made the son comfortable and continued on their journey.

After some hours of travel the father and the son arrived at their Mississippi Delta family home, and the down home family members were waiting along the driveway until the vehicle came to rest. When the vehicle came to rest the greeting begin with hugs and kisses with the son becoming the center of attention. After the greetings, a phone called was made to the ladies back home informing them of their safe arrival, before the phone call ended the entire down home family members got a chance to say hello and tell the ladies that they will be waiting for their arrival in a few days.

As soon as unloading the vehicle was finished the son went inside with the ladies while the father and brother remained outside. The father and brother took a walk about the property looking at the improvements since his last visit. The father and brother soon begin reminiscing about days gone by as they grew up in the same community.

"The father said, I can see the old house is still standing, which bring back old memories that should help to explain those scars that should still remain on your butt!"

"Yes , said the brother. There are some scars that remain on my butt caused by those buck shots of mustard seeds that ranged out from the double barreled shot gun of old man Burly that caught me in the butt as I ran near the corn field at the rear of his house, after being in with his lovely young daughter."

"Just as soon as his daughter and I heard some noise coming from the rear screen door, I ran out of the front door and around the house as fast as I could but old man Burly still caught me in the butt with those mustard seeds, and I wonder what if old man Burly had been using real lead buck shots; I guess half of my ass would have been blown away."

"I don't know what could have been, said the brother, but if old man Burly had been using real lead buck shots; I am sure that would have been a great reminder at each sitting."

"By the way Good Brother, how did old man Burly know that you were in with his lovely daughter?"

"Through the community news monitor, old lady Sissy."

"Are you telling your brother that you did not see Mistress Sissy before she saw you?"

"Yes I saw her coming down the road about fifty feet away, but it had been said that old lady Sissy could not see more than ten feet in any one direction."

"Just as soon as old lady Sissy reached the cotton field where old man Burly was working she told him that she had just seen a two legged coon sneaking out of the cornfield behind his house."

"Oh bye the way, how did you know that the sweet thang would be at home in the middle of the work week?"

"She gave me the green light at the Saturday Night's church picnic."

"At church making plans to be with the sweet thang soon, ha! Ha!"

"It seem like only yesterday, when I could hear our mother say each time that we went hunting; yall be careful and don't get shot in the butts, you here!"

"Little did she know that you were shot in the butt by a caring father after he had caught you in with a doll of a two legged rabbit young daughter."

"So much for me and the sweet one, how about bringing Good Brother up to date on the incident between you and your best friend older sister."

"All right my Good Brother, as I have said on other occasion that I went over to my best friends house, while his parents were away for the weekend; when my playmates older brother came out of the house where we were playing and said that the older sister wanted to know if I had ever been in with a lady that really knew how to please a man or in your case, a man like dude. I said to the older brother that I had never been in with any lady, but I had soul, the older brother went back inside and later returned saying that the older sister, Lu, Lu, was waiting, I went inside to find Lu, Lu, standing near her bedroom doorway, as she beckon for me to come over and the rest is history; because from that day onward it has been nothing but a desire to be with any lady of opportunity."

"Away from you and me, I am sure that you can remember a field hand lady called short haired Lilly, along with some other field hands that came to help weed our cotton field after we had fallen behind with the weeding after a few rainy days." "Yes, so called according to one of the field hand that sharpened the hoes used for weeding, he said that short haired Lilly once had long hair, but after one day she and another field hand lady had a fierce garment, hair pulling and scratching battle; short haired Lilly decide to wear her hair short and in braids; since short haired Lilly was constant during battles with the field hand ladies that chose to have an affair with her Straw Boss Husband, that day was not any different, because short haired Lilly and another field hand lady had a fearless scratching, garment and hair pulling battle; so much so until at battle's end, both ladies had very little on to hide their precious body parts and I am sure that you can recall the beauty under bodies that both ladies displayed, as all the fellows got some pleasing eyes popping views; of course, our eyes popping views didn't last long as our mother soon supplied both ladies with some clothing."

"The rest of the day we kept waiting for some more action, but every thing went smoothly and since we did not have any more need for the field hands; we did not hear anything from short haired Lilly, until one day we got news through the grapevine that short haired Lilly had left her husband and moved up north and she was operating a beauty shop, one can say that short haired Lilly was still pulling hair, but receiving good pay doing so."

"Good Brother I am sure that you can remember when our Pastor, the Good Reverend Jason life was snuffed out by his wife of many years, this was after she returned home unannounced after a short visit with her ill sister some miles away; Sister Jason returned from visiting her ill sister sooner than expected and caught the Good Reverend Jason in bed with one of the young church sisters, the young church sister jumped up and ran with next to nothing on before the good Mistress Jason could retrieve the gun from a dresser draw, however, the Good Reverend Jason was not so lucky, because his wife of many years blew a hole in his scull before he could escape; after blowing a hole in the Good Reverend's skull, Sister Jason placed a weapon in her husband hand and called the Sheriff claiming self defense, and after an investigation by the Law Enforcement, Mistress Jason was cleared as the Church sister was afraid to voice any opinions."

"Mistress Jason soon left the community and was never heard from again."

"Say Good brother remember when you and Tommy was located lying near that old whisky still upon Dawson Ridge drunk, and that was after finally being located by our father and a few other men in the community, our father had waited sometime for you to come home, before asking some of the men about the community to help him search for you and little Tommy, sometimes later they saw Sister Long and asked if she had seen you, she said that she had seen you and little Tommy playing near Dawson Ridge; and shortly after they discovered the two of you lying by an old whisky still sleep and drunk after having drank some raw corn whisky, the two of you were awaken after some cold water was thrown upon each face, each was later checked and declared alright health wise; but later given a few swat, which meant the beginning of a fun day going bad."

"I am also sure that you can recall the night when you got the family's car bogged in some of that Mississippi gumbo mud while upon lovers lane with that nice looking beauty from Kansas, it seem like only yesterday when I look out of the window to see the two of you looking tired and disgusted with some of that Mississippi gumbo mud clinging all over your bodies while approaching our driveway, after the two of you had gotten cleaned and relief from the long walk from lover's lane, you and I took the tractor, retrieved the family's car and cleaned it up before our old man returned; as we were lucky that our old man had left for church minutes before your arrival, we both would have been grounded for sometimes if the old man had been home and learnt about the car."

"It is time to bring our reminiscing to an end, because your wife has given the come and get it you guys, and Sonny Babe and I is ready for a meal since it has been quite sometimes since we ate, soon we were gathered around the dinner table ready to consume some barbecued chicken, southern style french fries, coleslaw, homemade dinner rolls, peach cobbler, soft drinks and coffee, and as the meal was coming to an end, Good Brother asked Sonny Babe to tell him about the spirits of creation?"

Before Sonny Babe could respond to his uncle's request, "the father said that the son should wait until after the first day's discussion before making any comments about the spirits."

Once the meal came to an end, the father and son gave thanks to all and especially to the lady of the house for preparing a good tasting meal and asked to be excused, because they were going to their room and get some rest.

Trip About the Community

Later that afternoon the father awaken and as he look out of the window, he saw the son playing with his female cousins, the father watched them play for awhile before asking the son to come inside and make himself ready for a trip about the community.

Later the father and son drove by the female cousins and waved as they passed.

The father first stop was across the levee near the end of an old deep cold and blue water hole where the father swam and played as a youngster.

"The father told the son that this was one of the places that youngsters came to swim and play when he was growing up in the same area and we would also put up an award for the first one to reach the bottom of the cold deep blue water hole, and after days of trying your father was lucky enough to be the first to reach the bottom and retrieve some sand and mud, and upon reaching the bottom your father as a youngster became so excited; until he tried to yell to the guys up top while sucking some water into his lungs, without panicking your father, as a youngster relaxed and floated to the top and swam to bank side, as a youngster I coughed and gagged until much of the water was out of the lungs and displayed the sand and mud that I had collected from the bottom of this deep cold and blue water hole."

"The guys congratulated me for my accomplishment and gave me the reward money that had been saved for the first to reach the bottom of the deep cold blue water hole, Sonny Babe your father's life was spared because of his quick thinking after sucking water into his lungs, however, many years afterward while on furlough from the military service, I chance to see one of the youngster from this community body being pulled from this water hole after drowning. It was a sad occasion for the community, and the return of a childhood memory when the father was knocking at the same threshold of death."

"It probably was the quick response by the father that allowed him to escape the same fate, and I have been told that its possible for an individual to be at the wrong place at the wrong time, or at the right place at the right time"

The next place of interest was the old rusty tin roof deteriorated house where the Langs once lived, the same house where Mister and Mistress Lang was married and shortly after their marriage Mister Lang met with an untimely death, months later Mistress Lang remarried and shortly after marriage, the second husband met his untimely death.

The death of two husbands in such a short time, brought suspicion toward Mistress Lang which caused a criminal investigation to be performed and once the investigation was concluded, Mistress Lang was cleared of any wrong doings, since both husband had been poison by a broken snake fang implanted in a boot worn by each husband, this cleared Mistress Lang of all suspicion.

We continued to the newly built house where an old house once stood that caused the death of our close female playmate, who met with death after she was believed to have been playing with matches, many individuals have met with their untimely death after playing with matches or some other fire apparatus, so Sonny Babe let this be a lesson not to play with any fire apparatus without the present of an adult or guardian with the proper experiences of how to deal with fires."

Our next destination was a return to our home away from home and upon returning we dug some worms for our fishing trip to the lakes the following day.

Once in our room we made a call to the ladies back home informing them about our trip about the community. To please the son, they seem very interested, since they had made the same trip before. Our phone call ended with smacks and kisses being thrown, and soon after Sonny Babe and the father played a few electronic game before retiring for the night.

FIRST DAY ON THE LAKES

Early the next morning the father was up at dawn checking on the weather before their trip toward the lakes. The father remained outside watching the farm animals go through their early morning routines before returning to wake the son and asked him to make himself ready for breakfast.

Sometimes later the lady of the house was calling out, come and get it you guys!

Soon and very soon we were gathered around the breakfast table ready to devour some homemade, pork sausage, hot cakes, scrambled egg, maple syrup, milk and coffee, shortly after we were gathered around the breakfast table, "Good Brother asked Sonny Babe to keep him up to date about today's discussion."

The nephew told Good Uncle that he will gladly inform him about today's discussion.

"Thanks said Good uncle, I'll be waiting," as soon as the meal ended, the father gave thanks to the lady of the house for another delicious meal.

The father and son returned to their room for a last minute check before loading into their vehicle. As the father and son was ready to pull away, Good Brother and his sweet wife was asking if they needed anything else after handing them a bag of goodies.

"The Father said thanks" and they were soon on their way toward the lakes and on their way toward the lakes they saw some farm animals having sex, but nothing was said; but from the expression on the son's face the father knew that an explanation would be needed at some other time.

Before long they were arriving at lakeside, and the father said that they should take a trip about the lake area before begin fishing.

They walked about the area as they observed many different animals and plants, as the father explained their functions, such as a different species of the plants and animals, and as they continued they saw a mother snake and her young's swimming nearby, as the son shied back and somewhat behind the father, the father told the son that there was nothing to fear because as long as nothing interferer's with her young's she will do no harm, the father told the son to take a look at the shape of the mother's snake head and to see that it is shaped similar to a triangle, which is an indication that she is a poison snake and be sure not to get to close to any snake with a triangular shaped head or to be more precise any snake with a head shaped like a snapping turtle."

They later returned to their vehicle and retrieved their fishing gears.

Once they retrieved their fishing gears, they walked along lakeside looking for a place to begin fishing. They soon located their favorite fishing places and began fishing.

Before long the father had to show the son how to throw and reel his bait.

Before long the son was casting his reel without difficult, this allowed them to have some fun fishing for the big ones and not so big ones.

The father and son fished for quite some time without much success, therefore the father thought that it was time for their daily discussion.

"Sonny Babe you and I is here today without the other family members because you are having difficulty understanding the duties of the eight spirits in the father's myth, written about in the writing titled, "SONNY BABE AIN'T NO MONKEY.""

"It is understandable since you have been taught only the Bible version of creation."

"Before explaining anything about the father's myth, you should be aware and told that the universe is larger than anyone knows about or understands it beginning, and long before its existence was discovered by scientists the universe have existed, how nor when the beginning became a living reality is anyone guess, and who or what cause the universe to begin will in all probability never be known."

"Yes there are many existing myths that gives the writer or authorship account of what might have occurred from the beginning, however, these myths are only speculative; yes the most publicized myth about how the universe had its beginning is only a myth by which its author might have envisioned, it is not for the father to say whether any myth is real or not, but like the father's, myths, are from the authors imagination, because at creation there was not any account of what may have occurred and any account given is speculative in reality, but who can say whether any myth did or did not occur."

"Should someone say to you, does any other planet exist aside from the planet earth, it will be impossible for you or anyone to know aside from the outer space explorers and since there was not anyone around to make a recording as creation took place; makes it impossible for anyone to know."

"In early civilization sailors thought that the earth was flat, and if their voyage went far enough their boat would fall over the edge and it took many centuries after the arrival of the human species before it was discovered that the planet earth was round."

"Let it be under stood that the religious doctrine begun only a few thousands years ago, when the human specie have existed much longer; then the question of what happen to the life after the death of the first human beings that existed upon the planet earth is unknown?"

"One must follow their own beliefs, because its their own salvation to save, however, according to scientists tech knowledge; the universe is over 4 billions years old and this is not to say that any religious doctrine isn't real in the mind of the believer, because one's belief is theirs to keep."

"Your father do not dispute any other myth about creation, however, your father's myth is different from most myths; since most myths have one creator, when the father's myth have the Eight Mighty Forces of Nature as the world's creators, because the elements are what each organism is made and survive from, take the elements away what would we have and this is why the father thinks that the elements were from the beginning."

"The first thing you should understand is the meaning of a myth, a myth is a traditional story of unknown authorship, ostensibly with a historical basis, but serving usually to explain some phenomenon of nature, usual, the origin off."

"There are many folk lore, which is a saying about something that may be believed, but may be just a saying, usual to send ones thoughts in another direction from reality, example the stalk delivering a newly born baby, when in reality the mother had given birth to that baby, the saying that if a black cat crosses one's path is bad luck, Lightning, God chasing the devil etc."

"According to one myth, the beginning there were only the water and darkness; Io, the supreme god separated the waters by the power of thought and of his words, created the sky and the earth said, let the waters be separated, let the heavens be formed, let the earth be; these cosmogonic words of Io's, by virtue of which the world came into existence, are creative words, charged with sacred power"

"The father's myth deals only with the realities of nature, and not with any one spirit as the creator.

"I will like to remind you, Sonny Babe, about the time when you came home with the question about how the world and its organisms were created, and was told by your mother and sister that people comes from monkeys and they also said that from your untidy look's made you looked a little monkish, and when your father came home from work and found you highly upset and later promised to write a different myth about creation, was at the time to make you feel better; and the father want you to realize that the reason that your father chose to write another myth, was not because you had been told that you looked monkish, but because the father had been contemplating on writing another myth since his early childhood, the fact that you were called a monkey was not the father's reason, because you have been called other animals look a like names before and that is normal for others to express their thoughts, parents or guardians also express their thought to others and children as well as adults will express their feelings, according to the American Constitution it is ones constitutional rights to express their positive or negative thoughts; however this is not to say that one will not suffer any type of consequences for speaking their thoughts, but they still have that right."

"If you or your playmates and other want to call you or you call them names, that is a given Right, but not necessarily according to the Mighty Force of Nature's Good, because name calling serves no good purpose."

"You were right to get upset about your sister saying that people came from monkeys or members of the ape family, because according to the rules of nature's heredity, it is impossible for any specie to create a different specie from their own kind."

"Metamorphosis is a change that some plants and animals goes through in their early stages of developments, however, the same stages of developments are repeated over and over without change."

"Your father can visualize that before the beginning of Creation there must have been gal-ores of elements, and these elements must have been organized by the spirits of creation the reason is like any thing created for future use must have some planning before being constructed, let say that if someone decided to build a bird house for example; then the planning on how and what that bird house will be built from is necessary, right!"

"Then in the father's view there must have been preparation by the spirits or deities with the supernatural power at the moment of creation to create a perfect world and its organisms which has lasted for generations after generations."

"Your father can visualize from the beginning there existed many spirits with supernatural powers to create our universe, and your father can also visualize that these spirits were part of the elements of wind, gravity, water, fire, life, good, evil and death."

"Before proceeding, we will now refer to the old spirits of creation in the father's earlier myth as The Mighty Forces of Nature, with the duty of creating a perfect universe."

"The word nature, means the sum total of all things in time and space, which includes the entire universe."

"Sonny Babe, don't get caught up in the spiritual doctrines; because these spiritual doctrines are associated with the teaching of individuals about eternal life, which is to give the believers a place of bliss after death, remember the earth existed long before any religious doctrine."

"The Mighty Forces of nature's creation written about by the father is from the beginning, it was the Mighty forces of Nature that had the supernatural powers to create the universe, because only supernatural powers could have created a perfect world."

"The Mighty Forces of Nature is the realities of living, and the religious doctrines are guides for teaching about the eternal life after death."

"In the real world the Mighty Forces of Nature gives to each organism the ability to survive whether that individual is a plant or an animal, and let it be understood that there were only two kingdoms of living beings, at the moment of creation, The Mighty Force of Nature's Wind had the first supernatural power of blowing and or moving each element into their positions in the universe that will last throughout the pages of time, and at the moment of creation, the Mighty Force of Nature's Wind blew each planet in the universe into their specific orbits, and remember that The Mighty Force of Nature's Wind is the most powerful element in the universe; as storms will prove and oxygen was needed to create a world of new organisms, with a duty well performed, the Mighty Force of Nature's Wind took its place in time forever, any one can say that the wind is not a supernatural force because I can feel its present."

"Yes! But can you see it, or control its movements?"

"Since at creation the planets had to remain in their specific orbits, the Mighty Force of Nature's Gravity was second in creation with the duty of holding each planet into their specific orbit; that was blown about by the Mighty Force of Nature's Wind, and with a duty complete without error, the Mighty Force of Nature's Gravity took its place at the center of planet earth in time forever; and gravity can only be felt but not seen, which means that only an unknown force could create the mighty force of gravity and the control of movements."

"The Mighty Force of Nature's Water was third in creation with the supernatural duties of creating the moisture needed to sustain future organisms; and with the duties of supplying moisture throughout the universe, the Mighty Force of Nature's Water took it place in time forever, and the oceans, rivers and streams begin to flow, but who can make H2O except the Mighty Forces of Nature?"

"The Mighty Force of Nature Fire was fourth in creation with the duties of spreading energy throughout the universe; and with the duties of supplying energy throughout the universe, the suns, moons and stars were glowing." "Yes one can start a fire, but not without the Mighty Force of Nature's wind and gravity."

"The Mighty Force of Nature Life was fifth in creation with the duties of spreading the seeds of life for the creation of future organisms, the Mighty Force of Nature Life took its place in time forever, and at the proper time living organisms begin to exist." "No one can create life without the male sperm and or the females egg and the Mighty Forces can create the male sperm and female egg, yes scientists can cause the male sperm and female egg to develop from a test tube, but scientist cannot create any artificial sperm or egg that will create a new individual, which indicate that it takes a supernatural force to create and bring a fetus to life; it also takes the supernatural's to create the chemical reaction in an animal to cause the excitement that can lead to sexual stimulations and gratification."

"At the creation of life the female plant and animal was created by the Mighty Forces of Nature, and the writer thinks that the very young should be taught about how to protect their bodies as soon as these individuals can understands the functions of their body organs, and as they grow also the facts of life, and with the lack of the proper education about the names and functions of their body parts, can lead to possible exploitation by the many predators that are waiting to take the advantage of the very young."

"The Mighty Force of Nature's Good was sixth in creation with the duties of spreading pleasant outcomes to future organisms, the Mighty Force of Good took its place in time forever; and at the beginning of life the forces of good outcomes began to flow, and good can only be created from the will power of The Mighty Forces of Nature, yes one can have good intentions, but it takes the force of nature to make them become a reality, because good thoughts comes from the forces of nature."

"The Mighty Force of Nature's Evil was seventh in creation with the duties of spreading unpleasant outcomes throughout the universe, and took its place in time forever, deception, ill treatments and bad outcome begin flowing; and it is the envy thoughts that causes evil deeds to be performed, like one against another beginning with lack of love for each other, good moral standards and the teaching of such is what tend to reduce evil deeds, and moral teaching is good for all."

"The Mighty Force of Nature's Death was eighth in creation with the duties of ending the life of future organisms, The Mighty Force of Nature's Death took its place in time forever and as sure as one lives; so shall one die, and without death, all organisms would live forever and if all things lived forever, there would be little room for survival."

"Sonny Babe before ending our discussion, you should be aware that the Mighty forces of Nature created the universe with both positive and negative outcomes, lightening strikes can be dangerous, but when controlled, will bring forth positive result-electricity."

"This will be the end of our discussion for today, because it is now time for us to have some more fun trying to catch the big ones and not so big ones, before ending our conversation, the things that you should remember about today's discussion is that the Mighty Forces of Nature was from the beginning, and their duties were to create a world for all living things and the Mighty Force of Nature's Wind had the first duty at creation of blowing the planets into their places in space, and the Mighty Force of Nature's Gravity was second in creation of holding all things with weight in place; these are the only two Mighty Forces of Nature that you will need to remember, because your learning will be kept at a minimal pace."

The father and son soon began fishing for the big ones and not so big ones and after returning to their places of fishing they had great luck and caught their daily limit, they made a call to the lady of the house informing her that they had caught their daily limit and they will be arriving soon; as the father and son was arriving the down home family was waiting to congratulate them, soon the lady of the house took the big catch as the father and son went to their room for cleaning.

Later after the father and son finished cleaning. The father and his Good Brother took another trip about the premise as the son played with his female cousins and as their tour about the property was about to end, "the father asked the brother if he still had the old single shot rifle that their father used to teach them how to shoot as they grew up in the same area?"

The brother assured the father that he still had the old rifle and had kept it in good condition, the father said, the reason for asking, because he would like to teach the son how to use a firearm since they did not allow the discharging of firearms in the city limit where they lived.

Soon after the trip about the property ended the lady of the house was calling out, come and get it you guys!

Later they were gathered around the supper table as it was referred to around these parts. For some beef patties with/ brown gravy, boil white potatoes fresh from the garden, green beans, baked corn muffin, butter roll pudding, soft drinks and coffee.

Once they were almost finished eating, Good uncle asked the son, Sonny Babe to bring us up to date on today's discussion, and the son said "that today's discussion was about naming the duties of two of the old Eight Spirits of creation, and before I discuss anything about the old spirits of creation, I want you all to know that the old spirits titles has been changed to the Mighty Forces of Nature; and nature was from the beginning; the Mighty Force of Nature's Wind had the first duty of blowing each planet into their special places in the outer space, and the Mighty Force of Nature's Gravity was second in the creation of our world that had the duty of holding all things blown about by the Mighty Force of Nature's Wind, in place, these are the only two mighty forces of nature that my father discussed today, and if there is any questions ask my dad."

"That want be necessary, said Good Uncle, because your explanation was righton in your good Uncle's opinion."

"Righton said the father, and there will be more discussion for tomorrow."

"The uncle said that he can hardly wait for tomorrow to arrive, because he really wanted to hear more about the old spirits of creation; or the Mighty Forces of Nature"

"The father said to the uncle that the duties of more Mighty Forces of Nature will be discussed tomorrow, and the reason for only two today, was because he wanted to make sure that Sonny Babe thoroughly understands the duty of each Mighty Force of Nature before moving on."

Once the meal came to an end the father and son gave thanks to the lady of the house for preparing a delicious meal and went to make a phone call to the ladies back home.

After reaching their room the father and son was soon talking with the ladies back home and after the hellos, the next question was how well is Sonny Babe learning the duties of the old spirits of creation, and the father stated that today's discussion was about the duty of the Mighty Forces of Nature as the old spirits are now called, and only two was discussed at supper; and the son did very well in his explanation to Good Uncle and family; we will discuss three of the Mighty Forces of Nature tomorrow, and if Sonny Babe's understanding is as good as today's explanation, we can be together much sooner than planned, great! great! Said the ladies all at the same time, other things of interest were discussed and finally finishing with the usual kisses and smacks over the phone.

The father and son played a few electronic games, and as usual the son was the winner and once the games came to an end, they took their showers and soon retired.

Very early the next morning the father was up and later outside making a weather check for the day ahead. It did not take long for him to realize that the day ahead would be ideal for any outdoor activities anyone may want too enjoy. He continued watching the different animal do their things until he decided that it was time to return inside to wake his son and ask him to make himself ready for breakfast.

Later the lady of the house was again calling out, come and get it you guys!

Soon we were gathered around the breakfast table for another good tasting meal and before the meal came to an end, "Good Brother, asked the son to remember to bring them up to date about today's discussion."

"The Son said that he would bring them up to date as much as he could, because things can be a bit confusing at times."

The father gave thanks to the lady of the house for another good tasting meal and the father and son was soon on their way toward the lakes, and sometimes later they were arriving at lakeside.

The father and son sat for a while and talked about how much fun the son was having without the other family members, but the father reminded him that their purpose of being here without the other family members was to give him a clear explanation of the Mighty Forces of Nature written about in his myth.

The father and son retrieved their fishing gear and soon begin fishing, they fished for sometime and having fun trying to catch the big ones and not so big ones, on occasions the son would take a walk downstream to play and throw flat pebbles over the water to watch them skip before falling, a few hours passed when the father thought it was time to began their daily discussion.

"The father begin by reminding the son that the old spirits of creation title had been changed to the Mighty Forces of Nature, and the Mighty Force of Nature Wind will be discussed again today, long before creation the Mighty Force of Nature's Wind moved in and about the huge mass of substances that was destined to become our universe and you must see the many planets flowing about under the power of Nature's Wind, when at the moment of creation these planets were blown or moved into their special places in orbits with the Planet Earth being moved in an ideal place where living organisms would exist; scientists agrees that the wind blanket the universe, which places the wind around and between each planet in space making them easier to be moved into their specific orbits, the father's myth, the wind was from the beginning, and in reality there is not any way to determine when the wind was created, but there was a need for the wind from the beginning for the planets to be held apart."

"As we should realize that all organisms must have air to breathe to begin and continue living, and it is a fact that an organism can live only a few minutes without the present of oxygen; a fact the wind is really that force that pushes the air from place to place, which is invisible and from the beginning the wind brought forth our different air pressure at different altitudes which is the reason why we have different weather fronts such as windstorms, hurricanes, snow, tornados etc., also the wind pushes sounds around and without the wind it would be difficult to hear different sounds and all the sweet music made by the different wind instruments, don't forget that the wind brings forth good and bad outcomes, and just think during a violent wind storm, one individual house might be blown away while another individuals home next door may not have received any damage; this is an example of a bad and good outcome and that is the realities of life, what your father is saying is that we exist by good and bad outcomes or if you like ups and downs."

"The wind as it is known is that force that pushes the air into the lungs of all living organisms which purifies the blood with involuntary motions and if an individual's lungs stop functioning properly, then their bodies will most likely begin to deteriorate."

"The Mighty Force of Nature's Wind fills the universe with oxygen and other gases need to sustain life."

"Sonny Babe if you and I would run up and back fifty yards, this would cause us to gasp for air, the reason being that we caused our lungs to be over worked and they will need rest before they can return to normal."

"The Mighty Force of Nature's Gravity was second in creation that was created to hold objects with weight in place as well as each planet blown into specific areas by the Mighty Force of Nature's Wind and at creation the Mighty force of Gravity was placed at the center of the planet earth where it remains, and without it we could not sit, stand or walk, and we could not have run from one place to another without the Mighty Force of Nature's Gravity holding us in place."

"The Mighty Force of Nature's Water was third in the creation of our universe, that was given the duty of spreading moisture throughout the universe and especially the planet earth, the precipitation is what brings us rain, sleet and snow etc., some water precipitation bring joy and some bring misfortune, water for drinking brings us joy while floods bring us misfortune."

"These are the only Mighty Forces of Nature that will be discuss today, because the father do not want to give you more information than you can understand and retain, of course these daily discussions are being recorded for later references."

"The things to remember about today's discussion is that the Mighty Forces of Nature's Wind, Gravity and Water are among the creators of our universe, the Mighty Force of Nature's Wind was the first creator blowing the planets into their places in space, Gravity was second that had the duty of holding everything with weight in place and the Mighty Force of Nature's Water was third in creation that had the duty of washing and molding our planet into their forms and brought forth the oceans, rivers and streams."

"Now we will again try our skills at trying to catch the big and not so big ones, we fished for a few more hours but without much success and decided to return to our home away from home; however, the down home family was not at home and the Father thought that this was the perfect time to teach the son how to use the old single shot rifle that their father had used to teach Good Brother and him how to shoot as they grew up, Sonny Babe since no one is at home, I will teach you how to use a firearm."

"Firearm, what's that said Sonny Babe with a curious look."

"A firearm is the weapons used by law enforcement individuals, like the Policemen."

Oh!

"Let's go over to that shed over there and get the old rifle and once at the shed, the father retrieved the key and retrieved that old single shot rifle that their father had used to teach Good Uncle and him how to shoot and the father said that this is a single shot rifle, and a single shot means that only a single shot is loaded at each firing; here take a look at it, and I will explain how to load and shoot it later, after looking at the old rifle, the son gave it back to the father.

"Back when your uncle and your father were children, it was customary for parents and or guardians to teach the younger children how to use a weapon in case the need to protect him or herself or a family member, or to learn how to use a firearm for hunting wild game, of course you are not likely to go hunting wild games, but there may be some other needs for knowing how to use a firearm; you should first learn how to load, cock, aim and fire before shooting it."

"Step 1.Take a look at the firearm or weapon, as you can see this is a single shot rifle, 2. Learn how to hold and aim, cock and shoot, the father placed a bull's eye target at the base of the same oak tree that they had used for practice on other occasions, and took the old single shot rifle, demonstrated each function by loading a single cartridge into its chamber cocked and fired at an old tin can that laid on the ground hitting it near the center; the father handed the old single shot rifle to the son and told him to practice its usage, and also told the son that he would give him a dollar each time that he hit the old bull's eye."

The son practiced each function and said that he was ready to take a shot at the bull's eye target that sat at the base of the old oak tree, the father gave the son a cartridge and the son loaded it into the old rifle chamber, aimed and fired, missing the bull's eye target by a few inches, Sonny Babe took four more shots at the old bull's eye hitting it three times with the last shot hitting it in the center.

"That was great shooting said the father, realizing how unusual it was for a first time shooter to shoot that well, never the less the son reached out his hand for the three dollars promised by his father and before giving him the three dollars, the father said that the shooting was excellent and it was unusual for a first time shooter to do so well, he asked the son if he had used a firearm before?"

"The son said that he had never used a real firearm, but he had shot his playmate's air rifle many times."

"That's why you have done so well shooting at that bull's eye target said the father and that it was unfair to give him the three dollars, since he had been using an air rifle."

"Pay up Dad, said the son, a deal is a deal, and his friend's air rifle was not a firearm."

The father reluctant gave the son the three dollars and said it was good shooting anyway.

Soon the down home family arrived and the uncle came over to the shed to see how well his nephew was doing.

The nephew flashed the three dollars that the father gave him for his good shooting and Good Uncle was told about the shooting and the promise made by the father.

"That was great shooting said his uncle, it took your dad and me weeks to hit that bull's eye near the center every once in a while, he then ask Sonny Babe how did he do so well on the first try?"

Sonny Babe told the uncle that he had used his playmate's air rifle many times.

The father agreed that it took them many weeks to hit the bull's eye and very seldom in the center.

"The father said that he was sure that Good Uncle could remember their first try, and that he had missed the whole thing on his first try."

"Good Brother said that he was lucky enough to hit the big barn house door on his first try and it took many weeks before he could hit the bull's eye regular."

They put the old single shot rifle away and the father and uncle played a few games of horse shoe before the lady of the house was again calling out, come and get it you guys!

A few minutes later we were gathered around the supper table as it is referred to as being the last meal of the day in the deep south, the meal consisted of deep fried fish southern style, mash white potatoes, diced garden grown tomatoes, garden green peas, fried apple tarts, ice tea and coffee, few minutes into the meal;

Good Uncle asked Sonny Babe to bring him up to date about to day's discussion.

"My father believes that from the beginning there were the eight old spirits of creation that he now calls the Mighty Forces of Nature that created our universe, it was the Mighty Force of Nature Wind that had the first duty at creation of blowing each planet into their special places in the world, and the Mighty Force of Nature's Gravity was second in creation that had the duty of holding the planets blown about by the Mighty Force of Nature's Wind; and the Mighty Force of Nature's Water had the third duty at creation of washing and molding each planets held by the Mighty Force of Nature's Gravity, and bringing us the oceans, rivers and streams, and these are the only Mighty Forces of Nature that was discussed today."

"Great! Said Good Uncle and he would like to thank Sonny Babe for a wonderful explanation about the Mighty Forces of Nature, and he would also like for each one to give Sonny Babe a big round of applauds for his explanation and his expert shooting, he is an expert shooter in my opinions."

The family members gave Sonny Babe a big round of applauds as he took his bauds, and said thank each of you.

"The father also said thanks and that the son had been a good shooter and had also given a knowledgeable explanation about the Mighty Forces of Nature, and he would like to thank the lady of the house for an excellent prepared meal, and it is now time for us to go and tell the ladies back home about how well Sonny Babe is doing."

As soon as they arrived in their room they made a call to the ladies back home and as soon as the greeting was over, the ladies asked how well was the teaching about the old spirits of creation going?

"Very well said the father after the explanation given to his Good Uncle and family." "I would also like to tell you ladies that your son and brother is also a good shooter of a rifle."

The ladies said great and then gave Sonny Babe a big round of applauds and kisses over the phone.

"The father then said to the ladies that since the son is understanding the spirits of creation very well, they can pack their bags and come on down any time tomorrow."

Yes! Yes! Yes! Said the ladies all at once and they will be down as soon as possible. The conversation continued for quite sometimes before they said, we'll see you tomorrow, and with the usual smacks and kisses over the phone they said good night.

The father and son took their showers and retired for the night, and after a pleasant night rest; the father was up early the next morning. He watched the morning news a bit before going outside to make a check on the weather for the upcoming day on the lakes and after seeing that the weather outlook was ideal, some more time was spent watching the animals do their things, the father then returned inside and awaken the son and told him to make himself ready for breakfast.

Later the lady of the house was again calling out, come and get it you guys!

Some minutes later they were again gathered around the breakfast table for some homemade pork sausage, scramble eggs, hominy grits, homemade plum jelly, wheat toast, milk and coffee.

As the meal was about to end, "Good Uncle asked Sonny Babe to keep him informed about today's discussion."

The nephew assured the uncle that he would be informed about today's discussion.

As soon as breakfast came to an end, the lady of the house

was given thanks as the father and son was soon on their way toward the lakes and once at lakeside, the father decided to take a walk about the lake as the son was soon fast asleep, the father saw some other guys that appeared to be dragnet fishing, which was illegal and before getting close the father saw them and decided to turned around and go back to the vehicle and wake the son, and they were soon at their favorite fishing places and begin fishing and they fished for about two hours before the father decided that it was time for their daily discussion.

"Today we will begin discussing the Mighty Force of Nature's Fire, that had the duty at creation of spreading light, heat and energy throughout the universe, and for the first time ever the sun, moon and stars were aglow, the sun is an incandescent star that furnish heat, light and energy to the solar system; the planet earth revolves to and away from the sun every twenty four hours each day, and some says that the sun rise and set, when in reality the sun does not revolve at all, the moon is a heavenly body that revolves around the earth once about every 29 ½ days and accompanies it in its yearly revolution about the sun, reflecting the sun light." "The star is any heavenly bodies seen as small, fixed points of light in the night sky, and energy is that force that has a capacity to work." "You can see that energy is a vital part of each natural force."

"The Mighty force of Nature's Life was fifth in the creation of our universe which had the duty of spreading the seeds of life throughout the planet Earth and any other place where life may exist."

"Before the element of wind, gravity, water, and fire, it was impossible for life to begin to exist."

"It was after the Mighty Force of Nature's Life created the seeds of life before the above elements begin to created the organisms of plants and animals."

"After the universe was created, later came the formation of each planet with the planets earth being in a barren state for a long period as the climatic conditions had to be right before life could begin to exist, and when the climate was ready the Mighty Force of Nature's Life created the vegetations, next the animals with the exception of the human beings, causing the planet earth to be in an environment of a chaotic state, because no animals before the arrival of the human beings had the ability to create and improve their environment, many centuries after the human species were placed upon the planet earth, it took many more centuries before they learnt the art of writing and many more before they learnt how to record those writings."

"Just think that members of the ape family was created long before the human being and they are yet to learn the art of anything except gathering food and caring for their young's, members of the ape family acts from instinct not from logical thinking, human beings have skin covered by hairs, while members of the ape family have a hide covered with hair."

"The Mighty Force of Nature's life created the method by which life was to begin."

"The method of the creation of life began with the sperm and the egg, the sperm is the male generative fluid, or any of the germ cells in this fluid, spermatozoon. Egg is the oval or round body laid by a female bird, fish, reptile, insect, etc., containing the germ cell of a new individual along with food for its development, and having an enclosing shell or membrane, or a reproductive cell produced by the female; ovum."

"The sperm and the egg cells is believed to be the beginning of the first generation of living organisms without any participation by the male and female, however, after the first generation, all future generations were created by the participation of the male and female of the plant and animal kingdom."

"The father believes that the first generation of living organisms were planted and brought into a living reality by the Mighty Forces of Natures without parents (sex between male and female) with the second generation being given the ability to reproduce by the male and female."

"Sexual participation between the male and female plants and animals begin equal from the second generation of reproduction onward, reproduction, is the process, sexual or asexual; by which plants and animals reproduce their own kind and Sonny Babe remember that without sex participation, life could not have begun to exist, or at least continued to reproduce and be aware that life is that property that allows an individual whether plant or animal to take in food, get energy from it, grow, adapt themselves to their surroundings, and reproduce their kind."

What is sex? Sex, is either of two divisions of organisms distinguished as male or female; males or females (especially men or women) collectively. Anything connected with sexual gratification or reproduction or the urge for these, especially the attraction of individuals of one sex for those of other.

"Gratification.—-is a voluntary reward for service; cause for satisfaction or benefit. The hormones in the average individual body cause the body adrenal glands to create a desire for sexual feeling."

"Sexual participation at first thought may be sex between male and female animals, however sex between plants most likely was the beginning of sexual participation, because food and shelter for animals began with the plant kingdom that also reproduce their plant sexually."

"Its impossible to say when the first life as we know it today came into existence, but food was essential for its survival."

Hermaphrodite– 1. a plant, or animal with the sexual organs of both the male and female. 2. A plant having stamens and pistils in the same flower plant, and different colors of flowers."

"The sperm and egg cell, is a very small unit of protoplasm, usually with a nucleus and an enclosing membrane; all plants and animals are made up of one or more cells, and the male sperm and the female egg in upper classes of plants and animals must be united before the beginning of a new individual, and according to scientific information the sex of the fetus in mammals begins at conception."

"Since it is impossible to have knowledge of Creation beginning, cause writers to create different myths about their beginnings."

"The myth of your father is that there had to be supernatural forces to create such vast space in which we live and have our beings and it was the Mighty Forces of Nature that brought forth the space in time for each, and the religious doctrines is believed to prepares individual for life after death ."

God is the state of being a god; divine nature; godhood. God-1., any of various beings conceived of as supernatural, immortal, and having special powers over the lives and affairs of people and the course of Nature."

"The father believes that at the beginning of life the Mighty Force of Nature's Life created the exact method of bringing forth the first living individuals by the union of one or more cells, and metabolism was apart of the first living organisms; metabolism, a term that encompasses all the chemical reactions occurring in the living organism, and cells is a very small unit of protoplasm, usually with a nucleus and an enclosing membrane from the male and female plant and animals."

"Their own kind is the union of the cell of the male sperm with the female's egg, or female egg only, with the two cells being united to begin a process of mitosis's which is the beginning development of the new individual; with equal numbers of chromosomes from each parent, the equal number of chromosomes from each parent will allow a developing embryo to be the exact duplicate of their parents, as an apple from an apple; an ape from an ape, as an ape male and female can only create an ape embryo and since members of the ape family roamed the planet earth long before the human species is an indication that the apes are only another animal whose beginning came long before the human beings, this is not to say that some humans do not resemble the likeness of apes and monkeys, but they are only look a likes."

"This will end our discussion for today and the most important thing to remember about today's discussion that from the beginning of life, the Mighty Force of Nature's Life created the way to begin living, but it took all the Mighty Forces to bring plants and animals alive and the male sperm and the female's egg is what created all living things."

It is time for us to again try to catch the big ones and not so big ones and once at their favorite places, the father fished for awhile before calling the ladies, because they should be arriving soon, sure enough an hour later the ladies called and said that they would be arriving within the hour, the father and son gathered their belongings and begin their trip to their home away from home.

THE LADIES ARRIVAL

The father and son arrived minutes before the ladies from back home and as the ladies were pulling into the driveway, Sonny Babe ran into the pathway of the moving vehicle causing the mother to stop in the middle of the driveway, as soon as the vehicle came to a stop the son was in his mother arms as soon as she open the door with the father quickly joining the mother and son as the sisters join them with kisses and hugs, by now the down home family had also joined in the celebration; at the end of the greeting and unloading the vehicle the son went with his parents while the daughters went with their down home cousins where they will stay on their visit, before long the entire visiting family was together talking and enjoying each other since they had missed being together for the pass few days.

The mother later went to the kitchen area to help the lady of the house with preparing and setting up the buffet lineup, as other members kept enjoying each other until the lady of the house was calling out come and get it one and all!

In a short time they were gathered at the buffet line, with the son leading and the younger sister right behind and once gathered around the supper table, they were ready to devour some meatloaf, potato salad. Cole slaw, homemade bake biscuit, blackberry cobbler, soft drinks and coffee.

Nearing the end of the meal, "Sonny Babe's mother ask him to explain the duties of the old spirits of creation."

"Alright my dear mother and family members it will be my pleasure to explain the duties of the Mighty Forces of Nature's Creation, as they are now called and there is no greater force than the Mighty Forces of Nature, and they are the sum total of everything, the Mighty Force of Nature's Wind was first in creation that had the duty of blowing each planet and things into their special places in the outer space."

"The Mighty Force of Nature's Gravity was second in creation that had the duty of holding all the things blown in the outer space by the Mighty Force of Nature's Wind, and with the greatest of force, the Mighty Force of Nature's Gravity held all things in place; and without gravity we would not have control of our movement from place to place."

"The third Mighty Force of Nature's Water at creation had the duty to bring forth the ocean, rivers, and streams and something to drink."

"The Mighty Force of Nature' Fire was fourth in creation that had the duty of spreading light, heat and energy throughout the world and without energy we would not have the sun, moon and stars, or hot food."

"The Mighty Force of Nature's Life was fifth in creation that had the duty of spreading the seeds of life, and without the seeds of life; we would not have any little ones, the seeds of life is created from the male sperm and the female's egg of both plants and animals and these are all the Mighty Forces of Nature that we have discussed thus far. Should there be any other question ask my dad."

"The mother said, that was a clear explanation Sonny Babe and I would like for all to give Sonny Babe a big hand of applauds!"

They gave Sonny Babe a big round of applauds and the father soon said that that was an excellent explanation and to the facts as he had explained. And then asked the family members to give Sonny Babe another big round of applauds!

They gave Sonny Babe another big round of applauding and as the applauding came to an end, the father asked each to give the lady of the house an applaud for such good cooking.

"The lady of the house said, thank you!" thank you very much!"

The family members went their separate ways with the exception of the lady of the house and the visiting mother. They washed and cleaned before leaving.

The visiting young ladies joined their down home cousins and Sonny Babe's mother father and him, went to their room where the father and son have been staying since their first arrival. Sonny Babe was given a roll away bed as his mother and father would be sleeping together.

"Later the mother asked the father if what the son said about the sperm and the egg was all that he had told him about sex?"

"The father said that there was more said, but there is even more that will be explain at another time."

After spending more time praising the son for such excellent description of the Mighty Forces of Nature they prepared themselves for bed and retired for the night and early the next morning the mother and father was up early, and later outside making a check on the weather. It didn't take long for them to realize that the weather outlook would be ideal for their trip toward the lakes, they took a tour about the property so the mother could see the improvements that had been made since her last visit and soon after the tour of the property, they returned inside to get their son up and ready for breakfast.

Before long the lady of the house was calling out, come and get it one and all!

Soon they were gathered at the buffet line with the son and younger sister leading and later they were gathered at the breakfast table for a meal consisting of some home cured bacon strips, scramble eggs, wheat toast, pear preserve, milk and coffee.

Before the meal was finished "Good Uncle, asked Sonny Babe to be sure to bring us up to date about today's discussion."

"The nephew assured his Good Uncle that he will be proud to bring him and families up to date about the duties of the Mighty Forces of Nature and anything else that might be of importance."

Once the meal had ended, they gave thanks to the lady of the house for another tasty meal, as the visiting family gathered their belongings and was soon of toward the lakes and before they reached the lakes, they saw a bull and cow having sex.

"The younger sister said to the son that the bull and cow was gitting it on and the sperms from that bull were sure to meet and penetrate one or more eggs from the young heifer that is likely to reproduce a baby calf."

There was no other comments about the sexual encounter, as they continued toward the lakes. Sometimes later they were arriving at lakeside.

The ladies soon took a trip about the lake in search for a favorite spot to fish. After a while they returned to the vehicle retrieved their fishing gears and later begin fishing.

"The older sister asked the son if he would bait her hook since she was a bit afraid of those creepy earth worms."

The son said no problem and he proceeded to bait her hook

and went to his favorite place and they each begin fishing for the big ones and not so big ones.

After fishing for more than an hour, the father decided that it was time for their daily discussion; as he asked the ladies to excuse them and the ladies said that they would see them upon their return.

A few minutes later the father was ready to begin their discussion, "the father said to the son, that the Mighty Force of Nature's Good was sixth in creation, that had the duty of spreading good and pleasant out comes throughout the universe and the Mighty Force of Nature's Good gave to each organism a new beginning which began at conception, which gave to all a chance for a full life span; Sonny Babe good out comes mean doing good which begin with the creation of the universe that brought forth a home, food and shelter for all living beings from the first baby plants to all babies around the world, with each organism beginning from the male sperm and the female's egg; with some lower classes of plants and animals beginning with the egg only and whenever one does good things for their neighbor and others is a true indication of the Mighty Force of Nature's Good have created a pleasant outcome, and good is from the will of others; both none and religious views; because there is good in the best of us and some good even in the worst too."

"The Mighty Force of Nature's Evil was seventh in creation, with the duty of bring forth bad, sad, and disastrous outcomes; which is evil at its fullest, and when you do mean thing toward your sisters, playmates and others, this is not the right thing to do."

"Be aware that good and evil begin long before any religious doctrines, since it took many centuries after creation, before any religious movement begin, however religion is very good for fellowship, and a chance to meet and greet people from all walks of life."

"It must also be remembered that the animal kingdom is believed to have existed billions of years before the arrival of the human beings, and many more years before the human beings learnt the art of writing, one must learn to accept religion from a belief in its teaching, whatever the faith."

"Evil or bad thoughts are not good but as long as these thoughts remain just thoughts then that is a part of living and if evil thoughts are not executed can never bring harm to others; however, continuous bad thoughts can become dangerous to ones body according to psychiatry teaching. Therefore, try to think positive about as many things as possible, because negative thinking is not good for the nervous system; be aware that if evil thoughts are carried out, then it will cause some form of evil deeds to take place, evil thoughts hurts no one but the thinker, and at sometimes in ones life there will be some evil thoughts about certain things when others might be going against their wishes."

"The Mighty Force of Nature's Death was eight in the father's myth, that was assigned the duties of ending lives in both plants and animals, and just think what would happen if every plant and animal lived forever; there would not be room or continue space to move about, yes we misses our love ones and associates when they die, but that is not a bad outcome, because their death is a natural way for continuing space for living organisms, of course it is a sad occasion but time will heal all things, so this will end our discussion for today and should you have any questions about this discussion please do not hesitate to ask."

They soon returned with the ladies and the younger sister had caught an eel, and was afraid to remove it from her hook. The mother had to remove it and calm her down.

She was still somewhat upset when the father and son returned and when the son heard about the incident, he begin poking fun at his sister until both parents insisted that he stopped.

They continuing fishing when later the mother caught a large fish that the father thought was too large for the strength test of her line and hook, but somehow the mother had reeled it in. They caught more fishes, but none as large as the one caught by the mother, until it was time to go.

On their way to their home away from home, a cell call was made to the lady of the house informing her about the huge fish caught by the mother, and when they arrived the down home family was waiting, waving and later congratulating the visiting mother for her catch and later calling her the queen for the day.

After the acknowledgement of the queen for the day ended the visiting family went to their rooms to clean up and after their cleaning they got together for their normal family get together with the mother still bragging about the large fish she had caught.

At last the lady of the house was again calling, come and get it one and all!

Soon and very soon they were gathered at the buffet line with the son and younger sister leading and they were later gathered around the supper table ready to devour some baked cured ham, egg cheese omelet, fried egg plant, homemade buttered biscuit, milk and coffee.

As the meal continued Good uncle wanted to know what really caused the father to write another myth, since they had been taught the Bible version of creation since childhood?

"The father said that since their early childhood, he had been contemplating on writing another version of creation, and you my brother should remember that I raised many questions about certain religious doctrines, such as why would an All Mighty God need to rest after six days of work, why did Cain kill Abel, and if Adam and Eve was White; then where did the Black Race come, along with their farm life being so hard, and the ill treatment of the Negro Race, with no mercy at all by the Majority Race Group; and many prayers were never answered, gave me the thought that God may not like my people either, you should remember when you and I as youngsters were given a trip to St. Louis, Missouri on the greyhound bus, and before arriving at the greyhound bus station in Cape Gerardo, Missouri, we had to sit behind the Jim Crow sign that hung near the rear of the bus; and from Cape Gerardo, Missouri we could sit in any seat from front to the rear, the reason was we had crossed the Mason and Dixie Line."

"Once in St. Louis, we later went to see a professional baseball game and when the game was over we decided to stop at a hamburger place nearby, and as we were about to sit down near the counter; we were told that colored were not allowed to eat inside."

"Hello!!" "Jim Crow without the sign."

"We did not pay for the hamburgers but Jim Crow was alive and well and that is one incidence among many that occurred over the years that was unfair to our Race, that cause me to think about writing another myth that would be fair to all, and beside there are many myths of creation written by others including the one written by Moses."

"There is that question from a religious view about treating thou neighbor as thou self, when seldom did anyone seem to care about their fellowman, besides Sonny Babe came home from school asking the family members what they knew about creation of the world and its organisms, this was another reason that inspired me the opportunity to write a different myth of creation that gives accounts about creation long before any religious doctrines were written, so please be aware that my beliefs are from an individual point of view and beliefs are theirs to keep or express."

As the meal was coming to an end, "Good Brother ask the nephew to bring them up to date about today's discussion."

"Alright my Good Uncle and family members, today's discussion was about the Mighty Force of Nature's Good which was sixth in creation that had the duty of spreading good outcomes throughout the world, which means that parents should take it easy on their children when correcting them and the Mighty force of Nature's Evil was seventh in creation, which had the duty of spreading bad and terrible out comes throughout the world, and we should not do evil things against each others; the Mighty Force of Nature's Death was eighth in creation, that had the duty of ending each life throughout the planet Earth or any other place where life might exist, and we should not be too sad when we loose a relative or pet, because death means more room for the living and this is all that was discussed today and if there are other question ask my dad."

Yes Sonny Babe, we don't quite understand the saying about death leaving more room for the living?

"The father entered the conversation saying that the son means that if all organisms lived forever, then there would not be any room for survivors, in other words the Mighty Force of Nature's Death duty is to help control space for each individual; so give Sonny Babe a round of applauds, because he was righton!"

The family members gave the son a big round of applauds, as the son thanked them and lady of the house was also given thanks for another tasty meal as they departed.

The mother, father and son was soon in their room with the mother saying that death is for population control and not for going to heaven?

"Yes, said the father, its for both reasons."

The mother, father and son continued enjoying each other before retiring for the night.

After a good night sleep, the mother and father was up early the next morning and they soon went outside for a weather check for a day on the lakes and soon it was clear that the weather would be ideal for fun on the lakes. They spent more time watching the different animals do their early morning rituals and later returned inside to get their son up and ready for breakfast.

Shortly after the son finished dressing, a short time later the lady of the house was once again calling out, come and get it one and all!

Minutes later they were again gathered around in the buffet line with you know who was leading and soon they were gathered around the breakfast table for some home cured bacon, scramble eggs, stir fried bell peppers, homemade buttered biscuit, jelly, milk and coffee.

"The Uncle asked the son to keep them informed about today's discussion."

The son and nephew assured Good Uncle that he would gladly bring the family members up to date about today's discussion.

At the end of the meal, each gave thanks to the lady of the house and each went their separate ways.

Later the father and family was on their way toward the lakes, and upon reaching they sat and talked for a bit before going to their favorite fishing places and after fishing for a while, the younger daughter caught a medium size fish and was congratulated by all except the son, because he told her as soon as she reeled it in that he was going to catch a bigger fish than the one she had reeled in.

The son then begin moving from place to place in an effort to catch a larger fish than his younger sister.

They fished until the father decided that it was time for their daily discussion.

The son had caught some fishes but none as large as the one caught by the younger sister and as the son walked by he told the younger sister that he was going to beat her upon his return.

Upon reaching their place of discussion, "the father said that the universe was four billions or more years old and its beginning is yet to be determined, one reason may be that the plant and animal kingdoms was created long before the human beings.

"The scientific study was yet to come and it took many centuries after the arrival of the human being and many more before any scientific data about the estimation of the age of the universe was made and one reason that the human beings were the last known specie of upper classes of individuals to be placed upon Planet Earth, may have been that the human beings would need food and shelter that was to be provided by the existing plants and animals kingdom and long after the arrival of the human beings, it would take much longer before they could learn efficient survival skills and even longer to learn the art of writing and much longer to learn the art of recording information."

"It is impossible to know how or when the universe was created, but in the father's mind the Mighty Force of Nature's Wind was the beginning mighty force that blew our planets into their specific orbits, and placing the planet Earth in the ideal place for the survival of living organisms, and after placing the planet Earth in its specific orbit, the planet Earth remained without any form of life until the temperature was suitable for life to begin."

Members of the Plant Kingdom was believed to be among the first living organisms, because the Planet Earth was in a barren state and would need vegetation to beautify and build a food and shelter supply for the coming Animal Kingdom.

Once the Plant Kingdom was ready to receive and sustain the Animal Kingdom, the first group of animals begin to exist upon the Planet Earth is anyone's guess, because it is impossible to imagine what group of species, the invertebrates or the vertebrates that may have been the first to begin existing upon the Planet Earth; the writer would guess that the invertebrates were the first living animals placed upon the Planet Earth because the first group of vertebrates would depended upon the invertebrates for food, the writer can also vision that after the arrival of the invertebrates and smaller vertebrates, then came the large vertebrates of many different species, except the human beings."

"After the invertebrates and the early vertebrates had roam the Earth for many centuries, then came the human specie that had the ability to think and express themselves within their own tribal groups."

"Members of the animal kingdom aside from the human being did not have the ability to think or improve their surrounds and members of the ape family included, because they did not have the ability to think either."

"After the human species arrived upon the planet Earth, they were later classified into three primary divisions: Caucasoid, Negroid, and Mongoloid The term Caucasian designates one of the main divisions of the human race, loosely called the white race, the Negroid is a member on any dominantly Negro people, and the Mongoloid race includes most of the people of Asia, Eskimos, Northern Americans, etc., who are generally characterized by yellow skin, and it should be understood by now that all human races were created equal; why! Because they all attend the same medical facilities except our ape ancestor, and x-rays indicates that all of the human internal organs serve the same function, receive the same type of diagnoses for the same medical problem; please be aware that only ones environment and equal opportunities will keep an individual from achieving."

"The Black Race of South Africa was venerable to the slave traders, because the Mighty Forces of Nature placed the many tribes in an isolated environment after the continental shift of north Africa from south Africa leaving them separated from the rest of civilization."

"There comes the question why? But it is impossible for anyone to know, but the state of isolation made them venerable for the exploitations by other races, that allowed them to be captured and brought to a new continent without any chance to escape; mostly because of the color of their skin, and it may have been that the Mighty Forces of Nature wanted to place them in an environment where their extraordinary talents to invent things to make life more pleasant for themselves and others, or was it to show their tenacious survival skills against so many arts?"

"Over the passing centuries, the majority race groups have tried to prove that the Black Race was inferior to them, however, there have been a lots people of color that have exceeded in all walks of life; there are many other members of the Black Race that have contributed to many environmental improvements like any other race, so Sonny Babe, please don't let anyone make you feel inferior to anyone, because of the color of your skin, because it's the contents of your character that can improve your life's worth.

"Race relations between races have improved over the passing centuries and it continue to improve each day, but it will take more time before the races learn to live together like the birds of the many feathers that will flock together, being reared in the

Mississippi Delta and on many occasions to see different flocks of birds eat grains and worms in the same surrounding without any outlining problems and in the writer's opinions we should be like the birds and at least eat together."

"It shouldn't be too much to ask the different race to eat together while realizing that once the meal is finished, each race can upon their choosing go their separate ways."

"It is a fact that the separation of the races over time have created fear of each others present to live in some sort of harmony, because in reality since we have been kept apart from each other, really mean that we don't know each other, so if we can learn to eat together in peace would probable make it easier to accept each other as human beings; however, the economic status in reality will not allow each one to afford some of the better things in life, which may be a reason not to fully except the present of each other fully, as most minority race groups have not had the same economic opportunities as the majority races because fortunately for them it was the work by the minority races that has given the majority race group much of their wealth."

"Yes there are many that will say that one should pull themselves up by their boot strap; yes that should happen, but in many ways there are no way to get the boot."

"Back to the slave trade cause by a group of tribes being at the wrong place at the wrong time, because the Portuguese later establish trading posts along the Atlantic and was among the slave traders in the early 1500s."

"The first Europeans to make contact with south Africa, was supposed to introduce religion, and the religious teaching and their associations brought forth knowledge about the many natural resources to be had for an exchange of cheaper commodities; but after the discovery of the Americus the need for slave labor became a profitable realities trade market that caused many Europeans to begin the human cargo shipments of young Negro slaves, usually as has been said, by getting the different tribal chiefs to stage warfare against each other."

"Later the Europeans and many others joined the human cargo traders that would last until the early eighteen hundreds when England put an end to the North Atlantic trade, however, the Negro Slave trade continued from South America after the North Atlantic slave trade came to an end, and there is not any statistics to indicate the number of slaves that might have been transported during the slave trade, however it were millions and perhaps billions, and this will end our discussion for today and the thing to remember is, that there are three classified Race Groups and many of our people was shipped to the Americas as slaves and was not partly freed until 1863 by the Emancipation Proclamation, which only freed fewer than 200,000 slaves."

"Please be aware that it took the Thirteenth, and Fourteenth Amendments to give the Negro people their Constitutional right to citizenship, however, it took the Public accommodation Civil Right Bill to allow Negroes to enter public establishments, of course one must be aware that it takes the will of the people to except laws with some assistance from certain law enforcement agencies."

The Thirteenth Amendment on January 31, 1865 is the document that abolished slavery. The Fourteenth Amendment on June 13, 1866 gave constitutional guarantee of citizenship and equal civil right to freedmen, and in effect provided that when in any state the right to vote should not be denied to any of the male inhabitants 21 years of age and citizens of the United States, except for participation in rebellion or other crime, the basis of representation in the state should be reduced in the proportion which the number of such citizens bore to the whole number of male citizens 21 years of age in the state. This section of the amendment, therefore, left the states the option between granting the suffrage to the Negro or suffering a proportionate reduction in the number of representative in congress.

"Mississippi was among the states to impose poll tax, before anyone could be eligible to vote, this was to discourage poor Blacks voters from participating in the voting process.

"The Fifteenth Amendment.- This decisive victory and the knowledge that it had been won by the advantage of the Negro vote in the restored states led the Republican leaders to ignore their recent platform declaration in regard to Negro suffrage. Shortly after congress assembled propositions were made to place the freeman's right to vote beyond the power of the states to change. To do so this by constitutional enactment it was necessary to make the provision universal, and congress, therefore, submitted for ratification the 15th amendment declaring that "the right of citizens of the United States to vote shall not be denied or abridged by the United States or by any state on account of race, color or previous condition of servitude."

The ratification of the Thirteen, Fourteenth and Fifteenth, gave the Negroes the right to be a citizen with the right to vote, however it took many sacrifices of injuries, and the lost of lives before many rights for the Negroes were finally allowed, the Rights to inter public facilities and later allowed to attend public schools after having the Federal troops protection for Black students to attend Central High, Little Rock, Arkansas and the University of Mississippi protected the Negro Student as he entered classes.

"Sonny Babe it has been a long struggle from Negro Slavery to Citizenship, for member of the Minority Black Races."

"Finally the Black Race have their first Negro President of the

United States which mean that the opportunity lay and await any Negro with the same opportunity if one applies him or herself."

"One can now say that the Negro has moved from the out house to the White House, since Colonial and early America; Negro house People was given a house out back of their master's house to cook and serve their master for his or her desire."

"It is not necessary for one to be at a high educational level, however it can be helpful to be affiliated with the right political party at the right time, but one must be intelligent with a good education free from a criminal record before becoming a politician and maybe the President of the United States of America."

"It is important to realize that any member of the Minority Race Groups will meet with stiffer opposition from the Majority Race Group and some of their own Race Groups, also mainstream America, and groups that are in control of the major" corporations; Nevertheless, one should never give in to any opposing force, because anyone can achieve if the will is great enough."

"So remember that only the strong survives against all odds, and personally the father would like to give the former Bushes Presidents for selecting the first Black Chief of Staff and two Secretary of States which along the chains of commands, any one of these individual had a chance to become the President of these United States of America. "Thanks Mr. Presidents."

"Now it is time for us to rejoin the ladies to see how they are doing."

Minutes later they were again with the ladies with the older sister displaying a fish somewhat larger than the one caught yesterday by the younger sister. Naturally the son became more anxious than ever before to attempt to catch a fish larger than either sister. The father gave the older sister a big hug and said that he was proud of all of his family.

They fished for the rest of the day with the son moving from place to place, but could not catch a fish the size of either sister. Even when it was time to go to their home away from home, the son was not ready to give up his effort to catch a larger fish than either sister. The son was the last to stop fishing upon the direction of his parents.

They finally arrived at their home away from home with the older sister showing them the fish that she caught, of course the son kept saying that if he hadn't been spending time with the daily discussions he would have caught the bigger fish, and tomorrow he'll surely catch the bigger fish.

The parents agreed with the son to calm him down with the fishing family going to their rooms to get ready for supper, the visiting mother got dressed and went to the kitchen area to help the lady of the house finishing preparing the meal.

Some minutes later the ladies were calling out, come and get it one and all!

They gathered at the buffet line with the son and younger sister leading as usual and later they were gathered around the supper table for some southern deep fried fish, scallop white potatoes, diced cucumber, coleslaw, dinner rolls, homemade ice cream, and sodas of many flavors, as the meal was coming to an end, "Good Uncle asked Sonny Babe to bring them up to date about today's discussion."

"All right my dear family members, today's discussion was about only the strongest survives, and a thanks to the presidents for selecting the first Black to positions that would allow them to be President of America, and that's all that I can remember."

"That's enough said Good Uncle, because that was clear enough for us to understand."

"The father said that he agree with Good Brother that

the explanation given by Sonny Babe was very clear and understandable, because we really discussed the Amendments that freed and gave the Minority Races and opportunity to become a citizen of the United States of America; that would be difficult for the average individual to remember, so give the son a big round of applauds."

They gave the son a big round of applauding as the son was saying thank you!. "Thank you very much, the applauding should really be given to my dad, because he has given me a clearer explanation about the Mighty Forces of Natures; I thank you dad and I would also like for us to give my mother and dad a round of applauds; my dad for good instructions about the Mighty Forces of Nature and mother for catching the largest fish."

An applauds was given to the mother and father, for their accomplishments, as both said thanks.

After the a recognition was given, the lady of the house was given a hardy thanks for preparing another good tasting meal; and the families went their separate ways.

The visiting mother, father and son went to their room and talked for a while and later retired for the night, because after tomorrow will probably be the last day of fishing before the trip to Vicksburg, Mississippi, before returning home and after a few more conversations they retired for the night, and early the next morning the mother and father was up early checking on the weather outlook for the upcoming day, they soon realized that the weather would be ideal for fishing on the lakes; they watched the animals do their things and returned inside to get the son up and ready for breakfast.

Soon the son was up and made himself ready for breakfast, and before long the lady of the house was calling out, come and get it one and all!

Before long they were gathered in the buffet line with the son and younger sister leading; and later they were gathered around the breakfast table for a tasty meal, and near the end Good Brother was asking the nephew to be sure to bring them up to date about today's discussion.

A thanks was giving to the lady of the house for another good tasting meal.

The nephew assured Good Uncle that he will gladly inform all about today's discussion.

Later the father and family was on their way toward the lakes, and upon reaching they sat and talked for a bit before going to their favorite fishing places after being reminded again that today was their last day for fishing, since tomorrow they will be leaving for a trip to Vicksburg, Mississippi and after fishing for a while, the younger daughter caught a medium size catfish and was congratulated by all except the son, because he told her as soon as she reeled it in, that he was going to catch a bigger fish than the one she had reeled in; the son then begin moving from place to place in an effort to catch a larger fish than his younger sister.

They fished until the father decided that it was time for their daily discussion.

The son had caught some fishes but none as large as the one caught by the younger sister. As the son walked by he said to the younger sister that he was going to beat her upon his return.

Upon reaching their place of discussion, "the father said that the universe is estimated to be four billions or more years old and its beginning is yet to be determined and one reason being is that the plant and animal kingdom was created long before the human species and only the humans had the brain power to think and create, also the human beings would need food and shelter that was to be provided by the plant and animal kingdom."

"Long after the arrival of the human beings, it took many more centuries before they could learn efficient survival skills and even longer to learn the art of writing and recording."

"It is impossible to know how or when the universe was created, but in the father's mind the Mighty Force of Nature's Wind blew the Planets into their specific orbits to remained in time forever."

"Although the Mighty Force of Nature's Wind blew the planets into their specific orbits, it took the other Mighty Forces of Nature to make it possible for living organisms to be created upon the Planet Earth."

"After many billions of years of growth the Plant and Animal Kingdom became a living reality, the plant kingdom was established long before the animal kingdom and continued to survive because their creation were for the support of the humans beings upon their arrival, since most animals would need the plants for food and shelter and before returning with the ladies, the father told the son to remember that no one know when the world was created, but remember that the Mighty Force Nature's Wind is the most important element in the universe." "This will end our discussion today, as it is time to return to the ladies."

Minutes later they returned to the present of the ladies and the son begin moving from place to place in an effort to catch a fish larger than the one caught by the younger sister.

They fished for the rest of the afternoon until it was time to end the day, but the son was not ready to go because he had not caught a fish larger than his younger sister; however the mother and father told him to end his effort to catch a fish larger than his sister because there is tomorrow and maybe he can catch the bigger fish.

Before long the visiting family was arriving at their home away from home.

They gave the fishes that they had caught to the lady of the house, with the younger sister showing them the fish that she had caught and poked her tongue out at the son. They went to their room for cleaning and after the visiting mother finished her cleaning she joined the lady of the house to assist with preparing of the meal.

Before much longer the ladies were calling out, come and get it one and all!

Very soon they were gathered at the buffet line with the son and younger sister leading and later they had gathered around the supper table for some fried chicken southern style, fried rice, slices cucumber, sliced beets, butter role, ice tea and coffee.

Just as the meal was coming to an end, "Good Uncle asked Sonny Baby to bring them up to date about today's discussion."

"All right good Uncle I'll gladly bring you and the family members up to date about today's discussion, Good Uncle and family members, today's discussion was that no one knows when the world was created, but the Mighty Force of Nature's Wind is the biggest force in the world and that's all that I can remember; so if there's anymore questions ask my dad."

"Sonny Babe was very clear and understandable, but not as long as we have become accustom too but let's give the son a big round of applauds anyway."

They gave the son a big round of applauding as the son was saying than you!

"Thank you very much!"

After the applauding, they gave thanks to the lady of the house for another good tasting meal and each went their separate ways.

The visiting mother and family went to their room and talked for a while and later retired for the night, because tomorrow was the last day before the trip to Vicksburg, Mississippi before they returned home.

The night was peaceful with the mother and father rising early and later outside making a check on the weather, for tomorrow they will be making a trip to Vicksburg, Mississippi, the weather outlook was ideal for their trip toward the lakes. The mother and father later returned inside to wake Sonny Babe.

Some minutes later the lady of the house was again calling, come and get it one and all!

Everyone was later gathered at the buffet line with the same two leading, and minutes later they were gathered around the breakfast table for some, pork sausage patty, scrambled eggs, buttered biscuits, homemade apple jelly, milk and coffee.

At meals ending, "Good Uncle asked the nephew to be sure to keep them informed about today's discussion, and the son assured all that he would gladly inform them about today's discussion."

Later the visiting family was on their way toward the lakes, when they saw the rooster chasing a hen.

"Look! Little brother, said the younger sister, that old rooster is chasing that hen to make an egg that you may eat, or if not eaten; the hen will sat upon the egg until a baby chick is hatched, and that is called reproduction, that was a good explanation of the way baby chicks and all babies are reproduced in some method from a male and female plants and animals."

Sometimes later they were arriving at lakeside and soon they began fishing. Before long the elder sister reeled in a fish larger than the one caught by the younger sister but not as large as the one caught by the mother.

They congratulated her with even the son giving her a fist bump, his competitor was his younger sister.

They continued to fish with a reminder that this was their last day of fishing, because tomorrow they will make a trip to Vicksburg and the next day they will be going back home.

Later the father and son began their daily discussion. The father reminded the son about the many sexual acts carried on by the many farm animals was one of the reason why he chose this area for their vacation so he could make comparison about the duties of the Mighty Force of Nature's Life of creation.

"Today we will compare the beginning of life as we know it to be today."

"In the beginning of the father's myth, life begin with the elements in which eight elements, the wind. Gravity, water and fire were the main elements needed before life beginning and continue growth of each organism as good, evil and death would insure control of each organism as they develop and survived from beginning to their ending; the father want you to understand that in life's progression only the strongest will survive, what is meant about only the strongest will survive is connected with ones environment as well as their abilities to survive within that environment."

"Remember only the strongest survive both in ones ability to defend themselves against their competition and the one thing to remember about today's discussion is that the strong will survive over the weak, and if you and another individual have a disagreement, the stronger argument or defender will most likely win the majority of the time, but also remember that it is not the strongest that wins all of the time, because nature is fair to all individuals and this will end our discussion and we will now return to the ladies and try our skills at trying to catch the big ones and not so big ones."

They were soon back with the ladies and no one had caught a fish larger than the one caught by the elder sister, so the challenge was still up to the rest to catch a larger fish, or the elder sister will be champ for the day; they fished until it was time to return to their home away from home, and no one caught a fish bigger than the elder sister, so she was declared queen for the day.

When the visiting family arrived to their home away from home the elder sister showed her fish and was given recognition and was call the queen for the day.

The visiting family went to their rooms for cleaning, with the visiting mother soon going to the kitchen to help with the preparation of the upcoming meal.

Later the ladies were calling, come and get it one and all!

Minutes later they were gathered in the buffet line with the son and younger sister leading and soon they were gathered around the supper table for some beef stakes, boiled rice with brown gravy, green peas, beets, lemon pie homemade, tea and coffee as the meal continued later "Good Uncle asked Sonny Babe to bring them up to date about today's discussion."

"Family members, today's discussion was about the beginning of my dad's myth about the wind, gravity, water and fire were the elements that brought forth the life as we know it today, and it took the Mighty Forces of Good, Evil and Death to make it worth living, because only the strong survived under the normal way of living, and that was all discussed today for more information, ask my dad."

"That want be necessary, said Good Uncle, because we all understand that in all walks of life the stronger individual will prevail with one exception of the wives; because they will prevail much of the time, so give Sonny Babe a round of applaud."

They gave Sonny Babe a round of applauds and the lady of the house reminded them that tomorrow we will be making a trip to Vicksburg, Mississippi for sure.

She suggested that each get a good night of rest, because we will be getting up early when the morning comes.

The lady of the house was also given a big round of applauding for preparing so many excellent good tasting meals. After the applauding, each went their separate ways.

Early the next morning the lady of the house was up early cooking and making preparation for their trip. Before long the visiting mother joined the lady of the house to help with the preparation for today's trip and soon it was time to wake everybody and make sure that they was up and ready for breakfast.

The ladies soon begin calling out, come and get it one and all!

Soon and very soon they were gathered around the breakfast table for some cheese, ham and egg omelet, with french fries southern style, with toast, jam, milk and coffee.

The trip to Vicksburg, was chosen by the father because he wanted to remind the children about the important reasons why the civil war was fought and about the Northern troops conquering the Rebels.

At the end of the meal each was reminded to make themselves ready for the trip. Some times later they were loaded and ready to begin their trip toward Vicksburg and after some miles of travel they came upon a shopping center with a miniature golf course nearby. Some of the family members went shopping while Sonny Babe his father and younger sister went to play miniature golf.

The younger sister was the victor, because she won the most

games before the shoppers were ready to continue on their journey to Vicksburg, Mississippi. One reason that the younger sister was the winner, maybe because she has been practicing the golf swing from her father's website www.swingitstraight. Com.

Sometimes later they were arriving in the suburb of Vicksburg, and the father suggested that they should visit the Civil War displays of the cannon used by the Confederate Army and once they arrived the father asked if anyone knew what was more important, to free the slaves or save the Union? Good Brother thought it was to free the slaves, but his sweet wife said that his main intention was to save the Union and again she was correct, because Abraham Lincoln said, that if he could save the Union without freeing any slaves, he would and if he could save it by freeing all slaves he would and if he could save the union by freeing part and the others left in slavery he would and the slaves were glad that the North won and President Lincoln did not have to make a choice.

"One other question, said the father, which Amendment freed the slaves?"

"The Thirteenth Amendment said the lady of the house."

President Lincoln, never had the chance to see the passing of the Thirteenth Amendment, because he was assassinated on April 14, 1865 by John Wilkes Booth, and one can only speculate what might had been if President Lincoln had lived to complete his term as president.

After a tour of the Civil War displays, the father, Sonny Babe and the younger sister went to play pool, while the other family members went shopping, the father won two out three from the son, but lost the first game to the younger sister; however before the deciding game was finished the other family members had returned and they went to the motel where they made reservation before leaving home.

The ladies spent the night together and the men including Sonny Babe slept in the same large room. The father and Good Brother played cards, while the son played video games until they retired for the night.

The next day the males were awaken about an hour before check out time. Soon they were on the road again and made a stop for food an hour or so after leaving the motel, after the stop for food, the next stop was at a relative house who wanted to say that God Created the Heaven and Earth.

The father did not disagree and told them to keep the faith.

They later made another stop by another relative house who did not say anything about the father's myth, and these were the only two stops made before returning to the down home family house to spend the night before going home.

Once back at the down home family's house, they sat and talk about their trip to Vicksburg, with the father asking if anyone knew that during reconstruction after the Civil War there was a Negro Lieutenant Governor of Mississippi, and does anyone know his name?

No one knew about a negro Lieutenant Governor or his name. "The father said, when the assemble in Jackson in 1876 impeachment proceeding were begun against the governor, Adelbert Ames; the lieutenant governor, A.K. Davis, a Negro: and the superintendent of Education, T.W. Cardoza and Governor Ames were allowed to resign."

"So you see during Reconstruction Negroes were allowed to hold public offices until, after the reforming of new State Government of Mississippi, then the Negroes could no longer hold a national political office until after many years of Civil

Right struggles and demonstrations and the loss of great leaders and it has taken many peaceful marches and not peaceful marches like the march to Selma, Alabama, sit ins, and Federal Troops to guard the first Black Students to enter Little Rock, Arkansas Central High, and Federal Troops were also used to protect the first Black student to inter the University of Mississippi, and it took the passing of the Public Accommodation Law, Affirmative Action and other Civil Right Legislature, before Blacks begin to gain more recognition as Citizen of these United States of America."

"Many prominent Black leaders and others paid the ultimate price of their lives before citizenship was finally granted to the People of Colored, and after such hard struggle; many Blacks will not take time to vote and or stay in school long enough to get a High School diploma, there is lots more to say; however, since we will be getting up early tomorrow for our trip home, this will end my talk and allow anyone else that might want to say something about whatever subject they might choose, but no one else had anything to say, therefore, they soon went their separate ways and retired for the night.

Bright and early the next morning, the lady of the house was up early and before long the visiting mother was up and out to the kitchen area to help prepare the last meal before leaving for home and the ladies was almost finished cooking before the visiting mother went back to her room to check on the father, son and the young ladies down the hall, to her surprise they were up making themselves ready for the trip back home.

Before long the ladies were again calling out, come and get it one and all!

Soon they were again gathered around the breakfast table for their last meal of this vacation, for some beef breakfast stakes, hotcakes, scramble eggs, maple syrup, milk and coffee.

"Good Brother, said that this is the day that we did not want to see come to an end, but this vacation has been educational for each of us because we have been reminded about our school days and more, because those daily discussion has been a good educational experience that shall never be forgotten, and special thanks to my nephew for such enlighten information, so keep up the good work, and it has been a pleasure to have each of you down here to enjoy; my, how time really flies by when having fun, so thanks for this time together."

"Next the father said, that he would like to thank his down home relatives for these few days of joy and it will be impossible to describe the importance of this trip, because the son has gotten a clearer understanding of the Mighty Forces of Nature, and that was one of the main purpose for being here and thanks to each of you for your hospitalities for these few days. Thank you! Thank You!"

"The visiting mother said, she would like to thank each member of this family for their effort to make everything the best that any host could make and I have enjoyed catching the largest fish and the time spent with each of you and with a special thanks to the lady of the house for those good tasting meals, thank you, and thank you again and again!"

"The son said, thank each of you and my parents, especially my dad, agreeing to spend sometime to explaining the Mighty Forces of Natures in a way that made it easier for me to understand and I have enjoyed fishing even if I did not catch the lager fish this time around, but the next time I'll catch the larger fish between the young ladies of my family and thanks to all of my family members!"

"This is to say that the elder sister would like to give thanks to each family members for making this one of the better vacation that I have ever had, and I am very proud of having caught the larger fish than my younger counter parts, thank you, thank very much!"

"The younger sister said, it has been fun fishing and seeing my little brother jump from one fishing place to another in an effort to catch a larger fish than me, I want to tell little brother and big sister that I am the better fish person, thanks to each family member for this enjoyable vacation, thanks!"

"The young members of my family are competitors, said the father, which is the way it was with me while growing up with Good Brother." "I would like to pay thanks to Good Brother and family members and especially the lady of the house, for all those great tasting meals, thank you, again very much!"

"Well said the lady of the house, it was my pleasure as well as my duty to feed my guest and especially my family members, of course, I thank each for their thanks, and we are hoping for a safe trip home."

The visiting family went to retrieve their bags and secured them for their trip home, and later the down home family members were gathered around the visiting family vehicles, as hugs and kisses were passed around along with wishing for a safe trip home.

Shortly the visiting family members were pulling away with waves and kisses being thrown.

After hours of travel, the visiting family was pulling into their driveway, as their neighbors waved while welcoming them home and after a long talk with the neighbors and at last the family members went inside and made a call to the down home family letting them know that they had arrived safely.

They again expressed to each other about how much they had enjoyed each other, until at last they said good bye.

"Before they retired for the evening, the father said that there will be more discussions with the son about the realities of life, and any family member was welcome to attend, however, each session will be recorded, as was all the discussions while on vacation."

Each family member said good night as he or she retired for the night.

The next day the father made some needy repairs around the property. The other family members did whatever came next, since they were out of school with no specific duties and daily events to attend.

The mother and daughters went shopping for needy things, and to do some window shopping for some back to school items and then did what ladies like to do.

Upon finishing the needy repairs about the property and cutting the grass, the father was now free for the daily discussions until time to begin his regular work schedule.

BACK HOME DISCUSSIONS AND RECAPICULATION OF CREATION

"Remember Sonny Babe, the Mighty Force of Nature Wind began creation by blowing each planet into their specific orbits, the Mighty Force of Nature's Gravity, was second in creation which had the duty of holding these planets in place, the Mighty Force of Nature's Water was third in creation which had the duty of molding, washing and supplying moisture for the planet Earth or any other planet where moisture may have been needed, the Mighty Force of Nature's Fire was fourth in creation, which had the duty of furnishing heat and energy for the universe and the Mighty Force of Nature's Life was fifth in creation which had the duty of creating living organisms; the Mighty Force of Nature's Good was sixth in creation, which had the duty of creating pleasant outcome throughout the universe, the Mighty Force of Nature's Evil was seventh in creation, which had the duty of creating bad outcomes throughout the universe, and the Mighty Force of Natures Death was eight in creation, which had the duty of putting an end to living organisms at life's end and this summaries the elements in the father's myth."

"Now let's go back to the time that you were upset after being told by your mother and sister that you resembled a member of the ape family, after you came home from school with a classroom assignment to ask your family members about their knowledge of creation of the world and it organisms, and when your father came home and later up to your room, and before leaving promised to write another myth about creation, and later wrote a different myth about the origin of the universe, one that would not indicate people deriving from members of the ape family, and over the passing months you had great difficulty when explaining the father's myth; the father later got permission from your mother and sisters to allow one week of the father's two weeks vacation time to spend alone with you to thoroughly explain the duties of the eight spirits of his myth in a different way."

"We spent about a week of the father's two weeks vacation time at the family's farm in the Mississippi Delta, and you were given a clearer explanation of the father's myth; however, today the father is giving another example of his myth titled, "SONNY BABE AIN"T NO MONKEY." From time to time individuals might say to you that they don't care about how the universe may have been created, then you must say that your father's version about how the world may have had it beginning is just another myth a long with other myth writers that have written their myths of creation that can be found in the ENCYCLOPEDIA BRITANNICA 1965."

"It may be impossible for anyone to know how the world may have begun to exist, but your father and other have tried to explain their beliefs about how things about them began to exist, and the father's version is just another myth among many."

"You might say that according to my father's myth, from the beginning the eight supernatural forces of the elements in which all things comes, was in the father's opinions the elements that created our world, and these elements were believed to be the wind, gravity, water, fire, life, good, evil and death; and the average individual might not care about when the world was created, since they are moving about in a spacious environment, with the sun in the morning and the stars and moon at night and that all that may matter to them."

"You might say, well to my father and others it does matter, and my father can imagine that there was the Mighty Force of Nature's Wind, the element that blanket's the universe and is the element in which all life depends for oxygen, and without oxygen there wouldn't be any life, water or any other element of great importance that allows all things with a circulatory system to have their blood pumped by the heart, and without water life as we know it could not exist, gravity is another important element that controls individual movements and without it things, literally would be floating about in the air; the Mighty Force of Nature's Fire furnish energy such as body heat, and sunlight, which life could not exist without, the Mighty Force of Nature's Life brought forth each living organism, the Mighty Force of Nature's Good brought forth each life with good will and positive outcomes, for each to survive, and to keep love and goodwill flowing and that make the world a nice place, the Mighty Force of Nature's Evil bring forth bad and unpleasant outcomes that brings us many disappointments and even death, which bring forth the Mighty Force of Nature's Death which bring forth life's ending to create room for the living."

"Now Sonny Babe the Mighty Forces of Nature brought forth life in a unique way, by creating the male sperm and the female egg, to create a new individual with equal numbers of chromosomes that allow them to create a new individuals in their likeness whether plant or animal."

"From the beginning the Mighty Forces of Nature gave the world both plants and animals a body with the human beings given two images, first the body and later the humans mind and or soul, (spiritual), the body and mind, as you may or not be aware that the human body is directed by the mind with the human beings reflecting on their own nature, it seems clear that each person has two distinguishable aspects, and certain of their qualities and activities belong to him or her as a physical body and are observable by others and in an obvious sense spatially localized, but there are also processes within an individual which are known to him or her that are not obviously connected with any physical part of the body; unspoken thoughts, wishes and feelings and since the unspoken thoughts, wishes and feeling are not part of the physical body, then it is the mind."

"When someone say's hello, you can say hello in return, or if you choose, you can say nothing which took none movement of the physical body; therefore, ones thoughts has little or nothing to do with their physical motion. However, it has been said that the thoughts of the mind can cause some physical harm to the body."

"The saying according to one of the religious doctrine, states that so as one think-eth so is he or she, therefore, one should be careful about their thoughts because; emotional stresses and worry about things that may be beyond one's control can lead to depression, many times individuals will continue worrying about something that might have been important that they were unable to solve, however they thought that their concern was important, when in reality it may not have been nothing to keep worrying about and an unsolvable event with no real answers."

"The mind can have many thoughts that are positive and negative, which each of us posses, and the mind has many definitions, but in reality, it is that force that controls an individual thoughts much of his or her life; however, there will be those times in ones life when their thoughts may not be clear enough to make the proper decisions."

"There comes times when certain responses may cause an individual to react positive, or negative, depending on their interpretation of the responses, example, if you are sitting and you were told to stand, you can stand or remain sitting; of course if someone yell fire! You would probably get up quickly without waiting for another response; your minds interpretation after the fire yell, said that it was time to move immediately, because from experience it knew the danger of fire so from this action and reaction proves that the mind control's the body."

"There will be other incidents that will call for a proper response from the mind that will be essential in the growth of the mind, especially the very young.

"Lets say that the IQ's have it.

"Let us take a look at what is important in our lives as we grow from childhood to adults, and a child should be taught reading, writing and mathematic to learn how to be an intelligent individual, of course ones aptitude have a great deal to do with ones ability of association with other and to be intelligent, one should have the ability to learn, retain and understand how to deal with everyday living, many individuals in today's world live by instinct, which is a natural or acquired tendency and the next two I's is intuition, which is the immediate knowing or learning of something without the conscious use of reasoning; and impulse, is another way some individuals act and react to certain situation which is a driving force or push for action and if an individual does not acquire a formal education, then that may lead to just existing rather than leading a productive life, and the beginning of ones intellect may begin as follow:

A STRANGER IN THE HOUSE

"Hello young lovers wherever you may be. It's a girl! It's a boy! Wait a minute, its both, and both are strangers to both parents although the mother thinks she knows a little about these little strangers and one thing that the mother knows which one was the biggest, moderate or medium kicker."

"The little ones mental development really begins well before they were born; knowledge of their development begin with the mother's report about their movements, and by the doctors observation from sounds and other activities given by the examination of the little individuals.

"In these little strangers, the earliest movement of importance were their heart beats which can be demonstrated during the third week, and at the end of the eighth week stimulation of their skin will provoke perceptible movement, vague at first but definitely localized later and, during the last three or four weeks, movement can be provoked by loud sounds, and experiments based on auditory stimulation indicate that something very like learning may occur even before the child is born; the parent didn't know this about the little strangers; the little strangers postnatal development, like prenatal proceeds partly by differentiation, partly by integration, and as a result of growth that has already taken place before the first cry; makes these little strangers fairly well organized, and before you know it the little strangers are rolling over, holding the bottle, sitting up and wait, he or she has made their first step; believe it or not you haven't seen nothing yet, because the table cloth with the basket of fruit is on the floor and just missed the little stranger with a bright look wondering why it was snatch up before grabbing that little kitten, I'll get that little fur-ball later, just you wait and see."

"Look mommy I am ready for school, but I don't want to leave my play toys that will never hit me back, oh well I guess I'll just have to pull a tantrum and maybe they will feel sorry and let me stay home another day."

"At five to seven years the little strangers are now rapidly acquiring a basic notion of the world of reality' their knowledge of the life as a human beings has been gained largely by imitating their actions in his or her play, but now, if he or she is not unwisely repressed, they will increase their fun of information by badgering his or her parent with unending questions."

"Junior stage.–During the earlier years of school life the child's performances in various directions are closely correlated, if he or she is bright, he or she is usually bright all around: if dull, dull all around, then come the puberty and adolescence; now it is time for those once little strangers to act like adolescents, whether boy or girl and adopt the code and attitude of others of his or her own age rather than those of the adults around them, this may bring attitudes that the parents don't really understand; however the now partly known new individuals still have the type of behavior that keep the parents wondering if they really knows the once little strangers, because no one can know what ideas lurk within the minds of adolescents."

"The parents keep wondering why some sons and daughters do what they do, even after they have done their very best to teach the once strangers to be the best that they hoped for and still some children do well while other keep the parents wondering where did they go wrong, when in reality the parent did very little to cause some of the action displayed by their once little strangers, the little strangers may have been influence by the outside world of drugs and cheaters with a greater influence over them than the teaching of the parents."

"So parents it may not be all of your faults of what path your little stranger may have taken because whatever will be will be."

Stages of Mental Growth.- Generally the time required for an animal to become full grown varies with size: a mouse matures in three months, an elephant in 20 years. No other creature has so long a period of childhood as the human being.

In general, however, an arbitrary but convenient method which divides childhood into three phases of equal duration is preferred. Indeed it is often maintained that a critical change overtakes the child every seven years, the close of the first being marked by the beginning of the second dentition, that of the second by the onset of puberty, and the last by the legal coming of age.

Each of the broader divisions is then commonly subdivided into two successive sections. This yields six stages in all: (1) infancy: (a) babyhood, 0-3 years, (b) early school period, 4-7 years; (2) childhood: (c) junior stage, 7-10 years, (d) senior or pre-pubertal stage, 11-14 years; (3) adolescence: (e) puberty, 14-17 years, (f) late adolescence, 18-21 Years.

"The above describe the growth and age of the normal growth from birth to late adolescence. Each human baby with normal developments will be as diagramed above. Your father was born prematurely but you had normal birth and fit the normal growth pattern."

"Knowledge of the development of the little stranger is derived from three main sources: (1) report by the mother of her experience of the child's movement; (2) observation of the little stranger by stethoscope, electrical, ex-ray etc. (3) the study of living fetus after removal by operation where examination of pregnancy has been necessary for medical reasons."

"The mind can have many thoughts some being positive and others negative, which each of us posses, as an individual is carried in the mother's womb, is not known to have any thoughts, however, at an early age the new individual will begin to response to certain gestures with laughter; and with more time the new individual will begin to say certain unknown things, the words are not understandable, with the exception of what sound like dad, dad, at least that is what many think, even those babies is without a dad around."

"It is important to note to you and others that it is important to think about the possibility of creating a new individual before engaging in any sexual intercourse, because the possibility of pregnancy means many days and years of caring for that child."

"The human baby begins with fertilization, the male sperm penetrating the female's mother's egg. The mother carries the developing fertilized egg and sperm inside her uterus until the fertilized egg (embryo), develops through a process called mitosis until birthed into a new environment."

"The new environment and the first breath of life is created by the Mighty Force of Nature's Wind, but prenatal development begins well before the child is born, knowledge of the development of the human fetus derived from three main sources: (1) reports by the mother about the movements of the fetus, or unborn child;

(2) Observation of the fetus by stethoscopes, electrical, X-ray and other modes of examination; (3) the study of living fetuses removed by operation where termination of pregnancy has been necessary on medical grounds and there will be years of of caring for that child before it can care for its self."

MIND–BODY AND OR VEHICLE

"Sonny Babe each human individual was given two entities of existence, the body and mind in which the father will call one's body a vehicle, with a positive and negative impulses which is controlled by the brain."

"The quality of the vehicle depends upon the quality of the manufactures, the parents."

"Let's take a look at the average new individual that is carried within the mother's uterus from conception to delivery and element of air is the first action that the new individual makes to set their vehicle air system in motion, the new individual is later given a chance to feel its vehicle keys, next a chance to hold steering wheel (milk bottle), next the new individual learn to sit and move certain thing on the vehicle, eight months to over a year the new individual learn to move its vehicle form place to place with the guidance of the parent or guardian; as time go by the new individual can move it's vehicle short distances from place to place alone and now the new individual has began to use its I. Q, a bit which stands for learning to operating their vehicle skillful according to its degree of intelligence, next the I-words may be instinct:- tendency to behave in a way characteristic of a stimuli, instinct:- to do or not do the right thing, intuition:-which is the immediate knowing or learning of something without the conscious use of reasoning; impulse:- an impelling, or driving forward with sudden force, sudden inclination to act without conscious thoughts and the usage of moving the vehicle intelligent will indicate that the new individual's I.Q is normal, which means that the new individual is moving in the proper lane of achievement."

"Sonny Babe it is important that you and your sisters learn how to drive your vehicles in the intellect lane since your IQ level is average, however, if you do not stay away from drugs and sexually transmitted diseases and hang with the wrong groups of individuals that can only indicate a life leading in the wrong direction."

"Now it should be the responsibilities of both sex parents to aid in the protection and nurture of the newborn until that newborn can be responsible for its self, and it is the duty of both individuals involved in the sex act that reproduced the new individual, to be sexually transmitted disease free for the protection of themselves and the new individual."

"Sonny Babe there is no excuse for two individuals to be involved in a sexual relation without protecting themselves from sexually transmitted diseases, and one should not be involved sexually without expecting both sex partner to be free from sexually transmitted diseases to protect themselves and the rights of the possible new individual."

"The father understands that sexual gratification may cause one or both sex partners to engage in a sex act without the thought of any protection for themselves or the potential new individual , however, any responsible person will not engage in a sexual affair without protection; because safety should be their first priority, get drunk, get stupid and have unsafe sex, which may be detrimental to ones self and others."

"Two individuals get together in a fun way that later turns romantic, so much so until a sexual intercourse takes place, but before the intercourse took place, did either or both sex partners think about the possibility of creating a new individual, doubtful, as it falls within a pre-sexual encounter, and due to the flow of the many hormones that usual a companioned the average excitements that takes place during the foreplay; sensible thoughts usually escape many participants."

"Now it should be the responsibilities of both sex partners to aid in the protection and nurture of the newborn until that newborn can be responsible for its self, and it is the duty of both individuals involved in the sex act that reproduced the new individual, to be sexually transmitted disease free for the protection of themselves and the new individual."

"Sonny Babe there is no excuse for two individuals to be involved in a sexual relation without protecting themselves from sexually transmitted diseases, and one should not be involved sexually without expecting both sex partner to be free from sexually transmitted diseases to protect the rights of the possible new individual."

"Now let us assume that each body is similar to an automobile that one might own; it shouldn't be that difficult for one to imagine that the operation of their body is similar to that of an automobile just purchased or given to one as a gift, and the human body is a gift from their parents and the Mighty Forces of Nature and at some point before the human body was created the parents got together willingly or otherwise and a sexual intercourse took place and the male's sperm penetrated the female's egg, causing the beginning of a process of mitosis to begin the reproduction of the new individual's body and or vehicle soon became a living reality that after many years of being over seen by the parent, the young new individual has learned how to drive its vehicle (body); although, the new individual have learnt how to operate its vehicle, the parent have the authority to advise its direction of travel, however, sometimes the new individual take the vehicle places that the parents would not allow if they knew where the vehicle was really going, and one example would be when the new individual is placing the wrong types of fluids in the cooling system, (drugs) and or parking the vehicle in the wrong places where it may be impounded by the law enforcement, sometimes the new female individual may allow some reproductive fluid to be emptied in the wrong compartment later causing a new individual vehicle to be reproduce leaving the parents disappointed but feeling obligated to allow the new individual to be parked along side of their used vehicle."

"Lets assume that before an individual (new vehicle) was made, both parents have bodies of good qualities, which will reproduce a new individual of similar quality and if the new individual is given quality care and protection, the new individual will begin life with an opportunity to be healthy and happy."

"Now lets say that one or both parent have a defective body caused by a sexually transmitted disease that will also cause the new individual body and or vehicle to be defected at birth, that may cause growth defects or worse death to the new individual, that will deprive the new individual him or her a chance or opportunity to live a normal life style, and the father is saying this as a reminder for you and your sisters to be aware of the sex partners that you might encounter as you grow and become responsible adults, because choosing a sex partner without care can lead to a life filled with sorrow and great disappointments, and it is not the father's intention to direct your lives forever, but it is important for you to be careful when choosing the males and females that you might meet in your life, to realize the importance of the possibility of the creation of a new individual before engaging in a sexual relationship, and above all be aware of the possibilities of contracting a sexually transmitted disease during the sexual relation, the lack of sensible thoughts can cause irreparable harm to all participants, and especially to the new creation of that stranger that may be welcomed or unwelcome to a new environment."

"Less suppose that these two sex partners were not you but some teenagers, but the care of the new individual must take place, why, because the human baby aside from the elephant takes longer to develop than other species and they can not do anything to help themselves.."

"Most teenagers and some adults does not have the means to take care of the new little stranger that may have just dropped in, now what if neither parent can not care for the new stranger that just dropped by, although the mother most likely knew about the coming of the little stranger, but she did nothing but kept the little stranger nourished for ex number of months; until arrival date; without telling anyone, now all one can hope for is that the young teen mother will tell someone at the time of birth, or else it might be a death sentence for the new little one."

"In today's environment, it has become necessary for the human beings to learn some type of skill to help with their means of survival, which means that both males and females should contribute to the aid and support for themselves and others that will be required to help with providing for their young's since the economic resources has been in decline due mostly to the decline in the natural resources. It is a fact that it takes some type of educational degree or special training in the mechanical industries and or medical to make the type of resources to support most of the very young; now let's say that the father appeared to be well finance, however, the father may have been a drug pusher, who may have been busted and is serving time at the arrival of the new individual, now who will care for the little one now?."

"As it is known that most jurisdictions requires both parents to contribute to the welfare of the child and sometimes incarceration may be necessary to get the support of both parents, and due to the heredity factor the proof is in the testing, but what about the parents being only teenagers and can not be arrested?"

"It is known that the hormones along with the pituitary gland secretion will cause the urge of sexual gratification in many individuals which may cause a rush to a sexual intercourse without any protection from the sexually transmitted, diseases nor the responsibilities of caring for the child.

"Now Sonny Babe, less say that one of the new parents were infected with a sexually transmitted diseases, and may have affected the health of the little stranger that just arrived, because both parent was not careful before the sexual encounter to assure that both were sexually disease free then the new one has to pay the price with pain and discomfort maybe for a life time, so keep this in your mind at each sexual encounter because the life to save may be the little ones."

"The new little ones mental development begins well before they are born, so keep this in mind; because the little one cannot talk on arrival doesn't mean that it doesn't have a body and mind."

"Now it time to take a look at the one and only thing that brings the sperm to the egg.

"**SEX.** Among the higher animals each individual is either male or female, in them maleness is the state associated with the production of spermatozoa; femaleness that associated with the elaboration of ova, and male is an individual that is efficiently equipped for the elaboration of functional spermatozoa and for the conveyance of these toward the site of fertilization; a female one efficiently equipped for the elaboration of functional ova, for the conveyance of these toward the site of fertilization, and often, as in mammals, for the prenatal care of the fetus and embryo for the nurture of the offspring."

"In certain groups maleness and femaleness are exhibited by one and the same individual either concurrently or in succession: such groups are hermaphrodites in both plant and animals, in plants is the different coloring flowers on one plant, there is some thoughts that a hermaphrodite is a homosexual; when in reality it is a plant or animal having both male and female sex organ and this is another way that the Mighty Forces of Nature created to replenishing the earth from the beginning.."

"Where the sexes are distinct, male is to be distinguished from female by differences in (1) the form and structure of the *gonads* or reproductive organs, those of the male being *testes,* those of the female, *ovaries:* (2) the accessory sexual apparatus of ducts and associated glands concerned with the transit of the products of the gonads: (3) the external organs of reproduction, and (4) certain skeletal, cutaneous and other less definite physiological, biochemical and psychological characters."

REPRODUCTION, the process, sexual or asexual, by which animals and plants produce new individuals. In so far as biologists have ever been able to discover, all life comes from pre-existing life (organic).

REPRODUCTIVE FUNCTION IN WOMAN

"During childhood there are no signs of activity in the female genital organs but at the beginning of adolescence (8 to 12 years) the ovaries are activated by the hormones of the pituitary gland (hypophysis) to begin the production of large follicles, which in turn secrete ovarian hormone, the latter is carried in the blood stream and stimulates development of all parts of the reproductive tract; in addition, the bony pelvis, breasts, hair and fat depots begin their progress toward maturity." "There is rhythmic alternation in the dominance of the hormones of the hypophysis and ovary, eventually the hormonal tides attain a heith that results in bleeding from the endometrial and the first menstrual flow occurs."

"Reproduction in females begin early and they get less recognition and bear's the burden of childbirth which the Mighty Forces of Nature placed upon them and not because of any specific reasons of punishment, since childbearing begin with female animals from the first groups of mammals long before the arrival of the human species, therefore, the writer of this myth sees childbirth by females as being from the beginning of the mammal kingdom and thanks to the Mighty Forces of Nature for all females; because inside the female 's uterus is to protect the development of the fetus."

"Sonny Babe remember that reproduction is the only way by which little one can be created, and this is done through sexual relation between the males and females; which is the only way except by asexual, and sex is no secrete but is treated as such by human, may be because of population control or the parent inability to explain without shame."

"The writer want to say because of today's expense of childbearing offer a bigger challenge than in the past, because, from the beginning the Mighty Forces of Nature provided the food, shelter and other needs to support the livelihood of child bearing and rearing; of course in today's world the expense of childbearing is very expensive, and it takes the preparation of both parents to be involved in the expenses of rearing the child since the human along with other animals have destroyed most of nature's supports leading to the great expense; but it is still the duty of the parents to support the care for rearing the newborn."

SEXUAL BEHAVIORS refers to all behavior through which the sperm is brought to the egg (q. v.). The mere existence of eggs, sperm and accessory reproductive organs does not ensure fertilization. There must also be behavioral tendencies and reactions through which the male approaches and inseminates the female. This is accomplished in so many ways that precludes a statement of the nature of sexual behavior of the different species has a common function: to secure the fertilization of the egg. Among different species of animals reproductive relationships vary from casual, without plan, promiscuous, without any care. monogamous pairing, together for life or as long as possible.

"Sexual behavior begin with the animal kingdom long before the arrival of the human specie and their mode of sexual behavior was the strongest male controlled reproduction, because the males would fight until one of the male was killed or gave up and took his chances elsewhere."

"In the human specie sexual behavior is out of control and probably has been that way from their beginning, because like other species, the human begin existing in tribal groups to insure their survival and at their beginning some male became the head of the different tribes within a certain territory."

"It is to be remembered that from the beginning that each individual begin without the knowledge and survival skills needed to survive in a wilderness of other animals, and from day one had to learn how to gather its own food; with plenty of competition from other individuals with the same intentions."

"Remember that other members of the animal kingdom already knew their ways of survivals forcing the humans to learn how to survive among all animals in the wild with nothing but his body and mind, the human beings were given the abilities to out think the other animals in the wilderness; because other animals only had the abilities to react by their instincts to gather food and as a group did whatever was necessary to survive and since the human beings are here today is an indication that we learned the skills necessary to survive."

"One myth would be that the human species begin their entry upon the Planet Earth upon an island without the most vicious group of wild animals, and with the passing of time; the human mind gave them the abilities of making the essential tools to conquer and rule their predators"

"Since sex was the only way to create new individuals, then the struggle to control himself and others, the human males learnt the skills of survival with the strongest learning how to control the weak including the females; this is not to say that the females were weak however, since they were assigned by the Mighty Forces of Nature, the duties of child bearing which was not any different from the other mammals females animals in the wild, it became the human females duties to conceive, birth and nurture the infants while their counter parts, the males, faced the challenges to protect and provide food and shelter for the females and their young's; this was not any different from other male and females of the wild, but the human beings had the mental capacity to rule themselves and other members of the wild."

"From their beginning the males of the animal kingdom was given the food and shelter to provide for their families; but over time the food and shelter became less and lesser, until in today's world natural resources are much lesser than they were from the beginning and has become much less, which is one reason why the writers have included the Mighty Force of Death as a method of helping with the population growth and survival; if death did not occur, then how would we survive.?"

"In today's world means that both males and females might be required to help with providing for their young's since the economy resources has been in decline due mostly to the natural resources, it is a fact that it takes some type of educational degree or special training in the mechanical industries to make the type of resources to support the very young."

"Sonny Babe when the father was growing up in the Mississippi Delta sexual behavior was under a different mode of behavior than it is today; as a matter of fact the time period was in the 1930s at which time it was a pleasant experience far the males to see above the females ankles and in the mid 1940s the dresses went up to the knees and in the fifties a little higher and to the mini skirt in the early `1970s, with today's length appears to be as high as one wishes."

"When the contraceptives of different kinds, brought forth a different attitudes about sexual behaviors, also brought forth more sexually transmitted diseases along with a huge population increase especially in some of the larger cities."

"After a new individual begin to learn the facts of life, that individual should in the opinions of the writer should be taught the responsibilities of respecting themselves and others, and that begins in ones own environment and the father have experienced young children being given drugs and alcohol that could cause ill effects upon these children, and parent along with others having little respect for rights of others in general; because they will smoke in the present of the little ones and others.."

"According to medical experts, smoking can cause irreparable damage to the respiratory system of many organs, so please beware, smoking is very addictive, because after a few cigarettes smoked while in the military, the father became addicted to smoking and it took quite a few years before kicking the habit; after trying to quit cold turkey, the smoking habit finally came to an end after begin smoking fewer and fewer cigarettes each day and about six months or less the craving for tobacco came to an end, let it be understood that the writer did not gain any weight as many may believe and the father have not wanted another cigarette since."

SEXUALLY TRANSMITTED DISEASES. comprise a number of contagious diseases that are most commonly acquired in a sexual intercourse. Included in this group are both a destroyer of life (syphilis, aids, and other diseases of mass destruction); an obviate of life (gonorrhea) The group includes at least four others diseases: genital herpes, chancroid, lymphogranuloma venereum and granuloma inguinal. These six are linked not because of similarity of causative agents, tissue reactions or symptoms produced, but because the principal means of the spreading of each disease is by sexual intercourse, especially promiscuous sexual intercourse, as implied by their name, "venereal." Not only are the causative organisms different morphemically but they also represent five distinct classes of morphologically but they also represent five distinct classes of microorganisms: spirochetes, cocci, bacilli, viruses and the Donovan body (perhaps a bacterium).

"Although much progress has been made in the control of sexually transmitted diseases, especially syphilis, and although the decline of syphilis in the United States has been outstanding, there is no evidence that other sexually transmitted diseases are declining; of course aids and herpes are on the rise without much chance of a preventive cure in the near future, and this should be a reason for sexual active individuals to become more aware of prevention before engaging in a sexual relationship."

"Speaking of sexual participation over time has cause newly sexually transmitted diseases to be created mostly among the human beings, for billions of years members of the Animal Kingdom aside from the humans have managed to avoid sexually transmitted diseases because they have been directed by the laws of nature."

"The human beings are believed to be the first animals to develop the sexually transmitted diseases because of their life styles, the human beings are the only animals that have the ability to develop cures for most of the sexually transmitted diseases but a few, and it is unfortunate for those that have contracted the aids, herpes, and other diseases without a known cure at this time in history and hopeful there will be a cure soon."

"The writer have attracted the venereal disease of gonorrhea, but learnt over time to use protection during a sexual relationship, and would like to offer some advice to the sexual active individual and or the ones that may be becoming sexual active to remember that the human beings are groups of individuals whose races were classified as three primary divisions: Caucasian, Negroid, and Mongoloid, neither according to the Mighty Forces of Nature is superior to the other physically; either male of any group can reproduce new individuals sexually, from either race group of females, only the mental ability may differ due to ones environments."

"There is not any moral standard according to the creation of nature, because any human male, a rapist, relative and others; can have sex consensual or otherwise with any human female, and once the male sperm penetrates the female's egg inside the uterus, the Mighty Forces of Nature directs each stage of mitosis until the fetus has developed into an embryo ready to be delivered into a new environment."

"Remember sexual participation which over time have caused sexually transmitted diseases to be created mostly among the human beings, for billions of years members of the Animal Kingdom has managed to avoid sexually transmitted diseases because as has been said they have been directed by the laws of nature."

"In many societies the very young are not protected as in others, however in both there are certain individuals that pray upon the very young for sexual gratification and these individuals comes from all walks of life because the urge for sexual gratification tells their mind to forget about any moral standards and sexually transmitted diseases that might occur at this time, so parents and guardians it will be important to keep a close lookout for the little ones, because they might need special care from sexual perverts."

"There was that time in the writer's life that gave him an urge for sexual gratification, because I was only sixteen when a beautiful lady from another community was visiting my neighbor next door; and after being introduced to such beautiful young lady, my unconscious thoughts and sexual gratification begin to flow and before the week was finished I found a way to have sex with my visiting neighbor, and I spent all night and into the early morning with the beauty queen from out of town."

"It had been the request of my parents that I was to be home by midnight of course it was past midnight and into the next morning before arriving home; naturally I told my parents a big lie in which they excepted, and about a week went past when my mother discovered an unusual spots on my underwear, and told me to go see our family doctor immediately, and after three visit the sexually transmitted disease was cleared, of course I was only sixteen at the time."

"My next sexually transmitted disease encounter came while I was in the U. S. Army I attracted a sexually transmitted disease from a street lady, and was treated by a doctor off base, and from that time until marriage I used protection; with the exception of having an intercourse with a neighbor without protection, but she was not infected and never again have I engaged in a sexual relation without protection."

"To each of you it is important to be aware that sexually transmitted diseases should be a reminder to any sexual active individual or that might be thinking about becoming sexually active, to remember that there are great dangers in during sex without protection."

"It is not my intention to direct your lives forever, but it is important to be aware of whomever you might meet in your life, to realize the importance of the possible creation of a new individual before engaging in a sexual relationship, and above all be aware of the possibilities of contracting sexually transmitted diseases during a sexual relationship."

THE ROLE of SEX HORMONES:-- The gonads (testes and ovaries) secrete hormones that have important effects on mating behavior and changes during mating season and many animals except the human beings that does not have mating seasons, of course the spring time season tend to bring about sexual feeling that may not be experienced at other times of the year, some adults in my State would say that the sap is rising."

SEXUAL DEVIATIONS, "Are ways of sexual behavior that replace normal copulation. Deviated conduct occurs in animals both human and non humans, and in human beings it may be out of the urge of a sexual experience not received in a normal intercourse; and homosexuality is sodomy; bestiality, sex between human being and animals; sadism, sexual pleasure by acts of cruelty, masochism, which appears to be the impulse to hurt others reversed onto oneself, voyeurism, obtaining pleasure by watching others undress or others having sex, exhibitionism, or sexual exposure, is exposing the genitalia to obtain sexual pleasure, so you can see that there are different ways for certain individuals to seek pleasure from sexuality, sexual behavior may sometimes, be related to intersexuality; which may be the mixing of the chromosome in the author's views."

"The influences of the chromosomes has caused the development of a calf to begin developing as a male and at some point finish developing as a female and there are other animals that begins developing during mitosis as one sex and change to that of another, however, as far as having been discovered or publicized intersexuality has not occurred in humans, but since there are so many human males and females being raised as one sex and later change to that of another; has little to do with homosexuality, gives the writer the thought that intersexuality might also occur in human."

"Although there have been other studies that may not indicate that the human beings sex changes during fetus developing, the father tends to think that there may be in some cases that the mixing of the genes might contribute to humans beginning life as one sex and changing at a later time to another."

DRUGS and ALCOHOL. "Drugs and alcohol may be some of the reasons that may contribute to careless sexual and other behaviors, because drugs and alcohol tend to make one lacked and less responsible about the thoughts of sexual behavior, get drunk, get stupid and have unsafe sex, which may be detrimental to ones self and others."

Drugs Addition, from a public health standpoint, refers to the habitual use of chemical agents despite harmful consequences that depend on the pharmacological and toxicological properties of drug, the personality of the user, the needs and demands of the society in which they lives, and the degree to which they neglects his or her own and their dependents' health and welfare through indifference or economic drain.

In the medically restricted sense, drug addition is synonymous with physical dependence, i.e., a state produced by repeated administration of certain drugs with the result that abrupt withdrawal of them is followed by physiological psychological disturbances (abstinence syndromes) that are usually transient but may terminate fatally, associated with the development of physical dependence is acquisitions of tolerance——-i.e., a progressive decline in degree of effect produced by a given dose of the drug; as the effect declines, the user is impelled to increase the dosage progressively, with the attendant hazards of toxic side effects and further intensification of his or her need for the drug to prevent abstinence distress. This cycle greatly enhances the habituation process.

DRUGS: Anesthesia and Anesthetics; ANTIBIOTICS; BARBITURATES; Penicillin etc. are drugs used to treat the physical ailments of diseases, however, overuse of these antibiotics.

"A reminder to each that drugs over usage can lead to addictions, because the more one takes, the more that the body will need to get the same effect; get high and loose your senses."

Drugs That Produce Physical Dependence.–- These drugs include opioids, barbiturates, certain none barbiturate sedative and alcoholic liquors.

In the medically restricted sense, drug addition is synonymous with physical dependence, i.e., a state produced by repeated administration of certain drugs with the result that abrupt withdrawal of them is followed by physiological psychological disturbances (abstinence syndromes) that are usually transient but may terminate fatally.

Associated with the development of physical dependence is acquisitions of tolerance——-i.e., a progressive decline in degree of effect produced by a given dose of the drug; as the effect declines, the user is impelled to increase the dosage progressively, with the attendant hazards of toxic side effects and further intensification of his or her need for the drug to prevent abstinence distress. This cycle greatly enhances the habituation process.

DRUGS: Anesthesia and Anesthetics; ANTIBIOTICS; BARBITURATES; Penicillin etc. are drugs used to treat the physical ailments of diseases, however, overuse of these antibiotics can be destructive.

"A reminder to each that drugs can lead to addictions, get high and loose your senses."

Drugs That Produce Physical Dependence.-- These drugs include opioids, barbiturates, certain non barbiturate sedative and alcoholic liquors, *opioids*.-- are those drugs that, regardless of origin, display morphine like properties; opium (q.v.) itself (containing 10% morphine and prepared from the sap of the capsule of apoppy, *papaver somniferous)* is usually smoked or ingested; morphine (q.v.) and certain of its derivatives such as codeine (methyl morphine) diacetylmorphine (heroin), dihydromorphinone (Dilaudid), dihdrohydroxycodeinone (Eucodal), as well as a number of synthetic analgesics such as hesperidins (Pethidine, Demerol, Dolantin), ketobemidone, methadone (Dolophine, Amidon) and dextromoramide (Palfium), are usually injected but are also taken orally while herion is often sniffed or smoked.

Opium is most widely used in the orient, while heroin is the commonest opioid purveyed illicity throughout the world. Though the effects of the various opioids differ, depending on the particular opioid used and the mode of utilization, the general features of intoxication and addiction for this class of drugs can be illustrated by the effects of morphine under experimental conditions by physiological psychological disturbances (abstinence syndromes) that are usually transient but may terminate fatally.

Coqueros," among the Indians in the high Andes of Peru, Bolivia and adjacent territories. The effects on the central nervous system depend on the extent that cocain is absorbed through the skin and membranes or on the dose if it is injected intravenously (the commoner practice of habitués other than the Andean Indians). The actions of the drug are ascribable to its capacity to mimic adrenalin and to stimulate the ascribable to its capacity to mimic adrenalin and to stimulate the central nervous system; as a result it cause papillary dilatation, rapid pulse, enhanced tendon reflexes, reduction of fatigue, elation, nervousness, insomnia, visual, auditory and tactile hallucinations (e.g., insects crawling under the skin) and paranoid delusions that may render the user dangerous; death may result from convulsions or from paralysis of the heart muscle.

MARIJUANA–– is a cannabis made from Indian hemp plant that is the source of the drug marijuana. Because of the tetrahydrocannabinol content of their resin, these products can cause congestion of the ocular conjunctiva, papillary dilatation, rapid pulse, dreamy states with impairment of time sense, loquacity, silly behavior with outbursts of inappropriate laughter and in some persons psychotic reaction. The latter are said to be especially common among inveterate users of hashish and if a new individual is not taught to respect its self and others, and those that say smoking pot has over time has realized many problems."

"**COCAINE**, is a white powder made from the leaves of a coca plant, and a large amount of cocaine come from Peru and

Bolivia, and cocaine is sold on the streets by drug dealers who add sugar; heroin and other substances to add to its volume, and cocaine was the thing until crack came along, which is addictive for most user on their first usages and some advice to the user not to use crack ever because you can get hooked and send your brains and heart down a path of destruction with little chance of a normal life style."

"Snorting cocaine was very common in the seventies and eighties in the west, and the writer says that because some of the snort persons play golf, and didn't seem to care if other golfers saw them take a snort, and later came freebasing that was a bit more dangerous, and then came crack in rock form and more addicting but cheaper than cocaine; however, depending on its user, since crack get one high much quicker than snorting and freebasing, which takes less time, then the crack user may spend more money getting high than the powered cocaine user. Some say not using any street drug is the best options, because drugs is dangerous to the health and very costly to the user; and once the body become addicted, nothing else seem to matter."

"Drugs users can become infected with Aids and other intravenous sexually transmitted diseases from sharing needles and other paraphernalia's and keep this in mind and try not to share needles and other paraphernalia, speaking of Aids."

What is AIDS, "AIDS stands for "acquired immune deficiency syndrome.

"It is for a cluster or pattern of diseases that come from the inability in a person's immune system that help the body defend against attack of viruses that will make the body weaker with a lesser chance to defend from other viruses, and when a person's immune system has been weakened or destroyed by AIDS, the person is vulnerable to many diseases that the body would ordinarily be able to fight off, but sometimes the person with AIDS also gets diseases that others might also get, but gets them in a more severe form than others; that eventually, a disease or combination of diseases becomes so severe that the person with AIDS dies, however, AIDS itself doesn't kill it only opens the door to diseases that will."

"Let's say that a person is infected with this AIDS virus, it lies dormant in the body for days, weeks, months or even years before any symptoms of disease occur. Some researchers believe that a person with HIV in ones blood has only 20 percent to 50 percent chances of getting AIDS, while others believe that people with HIV infection have a 100 percent chance of getting AIDS, sooner or later; this is just one area where knowledge is incomplete but changing rapidly."

"It's important to understand the difference between "having AIDS" and being infected with HIV, a person who has AIDS is very sick, and A person who has been infected with HIV may have no visible symptoms; however, either person could infect someone else, however, through sexual contact, sharing needle, or having a baby, neither person could infect someone else through casual contact, such as by sharing food or by a kiss on the cheek."

What Are the Symptoms of AIDS?

The First Stage of this disease is infection with HIV, and this stage has no symptoms; but about two to eight weeks after exposure, a person who has been infected with HIV usually starts manufacturing (*antibodies,*) the body's natural defense against a virus or other type of infection, sometimes, it takes up to six months for the antibodies to appear in a person's bloodstream, when a person gets a blood test to find out if he or she has HIV, it's these antibodies that the test is looking for."

How Can You Prevent AIDS? "Here is a list of suggestions for how to avoid being infected with HIV, as has been said countless times, AIDS is not just a problem for "high-risk groups, it concern anyone, gay, straight and anyone that do not try to protect themselves from sexually transmitted diseases."

"To one and all there is not a known cure for AIDS, but there are a few drugs approved by the Food and Drug Administration such as AZT, ddI and ddC that will help treat the infection of AIDS and help one to live a life of hope, however these drugs are expensive and the average individual may not can afford the use of these drugs, but if an individual would take precaution and use protective measures, that will lessen their chance of attracting the AIDS virus, and let it be understood that the only sure way to prevent AIDS is to remain abstinent, of course one can help with the control of the AIDS virus by using quality and dependable condoms such as latex and sheepskin along with spermicidal that contain oxynol -9, a female might use a diaphragm with jelly or cream that contains it, and a male use condoms' lubricated with spermicidal that includes this ingredient, or buy lubricant and put some inside the condom and avoid anal sex, fitting, rimming, or an activity that puts one in contact with a sex partners blood, feces or urine, don't share needles of any kind, and avoid open-mouth kissing with any known affected individual, and be sure to use condom or a diaphragm to help with the control of contracting any sexually transmitted disease.

"Genital Herpes, is a common sexually transmitted disease with many cases reported in the U.S. each year, it takes the form of cold sores in the genital area and these sores usually appears within ten days of the infection and heal within about three weeks, after that the infected person can experience a flare-up of the sore at any times; and the first attack is worst, which usually follows sexual contact, oral, anal or genital with the individual that was recovering from a herpes attack, a woman develops a small itchy area inside her labia, and a man develops a small itchy area on the shaft of his penis; while some individuals get headaches with the attack, while others might just feel sick, or as though they are getting the flu, and about 24 hours the itchy area develops small reddish bumps that turn into blisters by the following day, generally, the area is tender and painful; the woman's labia may become so swollen that it hurt for her to urinate, eventually, the blisters burst, leaving behind ulcers or sores, as the sores scab over in four or so days, and after a week or two has passed, they are usually completely healed; However, during the healing process and about a week after, the virus is very easily spread from the infected, and if a person's mouth or genitals touch the infected area, that person is likely to get herpes."

"Another danger with genital herpes sores is that they might be scratched with a hand that would then touch a person's eye, raising the possibility that the blisters and ulcers would seriously damage the eye, to prevent this, a person with herpes sores should wear underpants to bed, to prevent scratching the sores during the night."

"There are other procedures that may be followed, but the biggest danger associated with herpes is the unborn and new little ones mothers with herpes, and if a child is born while a mother's sores are active, the baby has a 50–50 chance of getting herpes; two-thirds of the babies who get herpes at birth die, about half of the ones that survives suffer permanent brain or eye damage."

"If you or your partner is suffering from a herpes attack, you may be able to see it if you know what to look for, however, sores can also occur inside a woman where they are not visible and she is still infectious for the week after the sores heal; and may be infectious other times as well, furthermore, a person might pass along the herpes virus unknowingly, and without having had a serious enough herpes attack to realize that he or she has the virus and remember protection before gratification is safer."

"Herpes infections are high and easy to spread, one reason being that some time the infected individual may not realize that they are infected since there are no visible sign of infection, however, if condoms and other precautionary steps are followed; may lessen ones chances.")

Pelvic Inflammatory disease (PID)

The pelvis is the lower part of the body, that includes the internal and eternal sexual organs. Pelvic inflammatory disease affects only women, although they may get the disease as the result of infections or diseases that men have.

PID is actually not a single disease, but rather a complication that can result from other diseases, including sexually transmitted ones. In fact, PID is the most frequent complication that women experience from STDs. The term PID means any of infection that gets into a woman's fallopian tubes, ovaries, uterus, or some combination of those organs. Because the kinds of organisms that can infect these parts of a woman's body are often passed through sex, PID is considered a sexually transmitted disease. What that means is that if a woman develops PID, she needs to make sure that her sexual partners are tested and treated for any conditions they may have that are infecting her, so it is very important that sexual active individuals be aware of all infections that may occur in the lower area of their body and never try to treat them using home type cures."

"Sonny Babe and family do not forget that all new human individual begins life as a baby that can not care for its self before their late teens, only the elephant baby takes longer to become an adult, of course, your father and mother have taught you and your sisters how to care and protect your bodies; along with the responsibilities of every day life, and above all the responsibilities to respect others."

"Over the passing of time it was discovered that the females were to carry and deliver the new individuals and once the new individuals arrived, the male and female new that some care had to be given to the little ones, the humans from the beginning were like that of any other mammal without shame when having sex; however, over time the human minds taught them to respect the present of others, and what time in the course of civilization that the human being began to think about sex as being a private affair is anyone's guess, but we are aware that it has been quite some time ago since the humans begin treating a sexual relation as a private affair."

"Sonny Babe as you can see that the farm animals did not treat sex as a secret and the reason may be because animals aside from the humans only have instinct and sexual gratification, of course animals do not have indoor private facilities so wherever is as good as any, and sexual behavior in humans are quite different because they have a mind that teach them to act in private as a whole, the young males are not taught to be as careful as the females about under body exposure because females are venerable to sexual exploitation; however in today's world the young males should be careful also, since there are so many perverts, all young males should be taught to protect their lower bodies also; so it is the fathers and mothers duties to inform their family members to think about ones action before engaging in a sexual encounter that may affect their bodies, information coming from the parents should be given, but some parents sexually abuse their children also."

"Now you may learn about drugs from your classmates and others. Especially since there are a lot of drugs on the street, school and many other places, even the drugs prescribed to many adults is being stolen by drug users of all ages, therefore it is a good idea for each to watch their prescribed medication."

"The father was taking a class in a mental enrichment program for adults, and one of the adult said that their was a young individual that asked to use the bathroom for emergency reasons, and after a few visit by the emergency user; the owner discovered that some prescribed medication was missing, and this type of experience has been realize by many seniors, so don't let anyone teach you to use any type of drugs, because prescription and illicit drugs are sold by drug dealers and other; usually for money."

"An individual may say that its alright to try anything once especially drugs and this may not be beneficial because it only takes a few usage to get started and there are crack cocaine and other drugs that requires only one usage to become hooked.

"To the family members and to anyone that may read this writing, the writer would like to wish each a pleasant read.

CREATION, MYTHS OF. Myth, in primitive society, does not represent abstract philosophizing concerning the ultimate origin of the universe, or the beginning and essential nature of humans; nor, indeed, is it a fanciful explanation of how the universe came into existence (as was formerly supposed), though fictitious incidents may be recorded frequently in the narrative. The primitive mind considers that things are as they are because they have been so created and ordained, and primitive interest in the past course of events is centered upon their bearing on present affairs and realities. This is demonstrated in myth by the belief that the spoken word is an oracle, and that the repetition of the word sets free the creative and re-creative power with which it is replete."

"Thus, the numerous myths of origin which recur in primitive states of culture throughout the world are not the expression of an innate inquisitiveness about the problem of creation, an intellectual search for a "first" cause" such as occupied the minds of the Ionian thinkers. Neither are they imaginative episodes such as Plato employed to give a clearer vision of the truth they were intended to convey, and to fill a gap in philosophical reasoning and empirical knowledge. Primitive myths originate from the conviction that the creation of the world had a permanent effect on subsequent behavior and on the structure of society. Thus among the Australian aborigines, the mythic past is concerned largely with the dream time of long ago," the Alcheringa, when the ancestors brought the existing configuration of the country into being, created the various human groups and ordered their laws, customs, belief and the social and religious organization before they retired to the sky-world. What was then initiated has to be enacted by their descendants in the prescribed cultus because the well-being of the tribe depends upon the repetition of the events in the creative period. So the myth lives on in its ritual, and the creative process is an ever-present reality giving stability to the social structure and institutions."

"The problem of ultimate origins and the idea of creation *xenophile* lie outside the range of the primitive mind; in cosmological myth all things are assumed usually to have been created from an existing order, such as a primeval ocean. According to one of the myth of the Crow Indian of Montana, for instance, long ago there was only water in which were ducks. Then the Sun as the creator, who has become merged with the "transformer" known as the Coyote, told them to dive into the water and from the mud on the webbed feet of one of them he created the earth and peopled it with living creatures. This episode is a typical example of the cycle of creation stories associated with th Sun-Coyote as a "transformer" in the myths of the Crow and of the Thompson River Indians of British Columbia. They have parallels throughout the new world, the cosmological myths in southern and eastern Australia, in Africa and the Pacific . In these myths the problem of a beginning in time or of time never occurs in the sense in which it has vexed the minds of later sophisticated thinkers. Creation centers in the production of the earth in its present form and the way it was made habitable and serviceable for human beings."

"Do not forget that all new human individual begins life as a baby that can not care for its self before their late teens, only the elephant baby takes longer to become an adult, of course, your father and mother has taught you and your sisters how to care and protect your bodies; along with the responsibilities of every day life, and above all the responsibilities to respect others."

"Over the passing of time it was discovered that the females were to carry and deliver the new individuals and once the new individuals arrived, the male and female knew that some care had to be given to the little ones, the humans from the beginning were like that of any other mammal without shame when having sex; however, over time the human minds taught them to respect the present of others, and what time in the course of civilization that the human being began to think about sex as being a private affair is anyone's guess, but we are aware that it has been quite some time ago since the humans begin treating a sexual relation as a private affair."

"Sonny Babe as you can see that the farm animals did not treat sex as a secret and the reason may be because animals aside from the humans have only one thing in view and that is to satisfy their sexual gratification, which later creates the new individuals that in some will care for their young's for a period of time."

"Sexual behavior in humans are quite different because they have a mind that teach them to act in private as a whole, the young males are not taught to be as careful as the females about under body exposure because females are venerable to sexual exploitation; however in today's world the young male may be venerable also, since there are so many perverts, the young males should be taught to protect their lower bodies also.

"Remember that the body is to houses the vital organs that sustain the body's physical makeup, and the body is the physical portion that allow you to stand, sit or walk, with muscle and ligaments to move the body parts, and then a mind to operate the physical body, what is so far known plants does not have a mind; only the humans has a mind with other animals having instincts."

"The mind is connected with the mental portion of the physical body and at one's parting, only the religious soul is to receive a resting place throughout eternity."

"The humans can have a spiritual soul once the mind become connected with spirituality and the soul is not connected until one' final bliss, however, the mental aspect can be taught how the eternal bliss may be acquired."

"Your body is ones most pride possession and it begins at conception and its growth rest with the Mighty Forces of Nature."

"If there is some type of physical body defect for whatever reasons that do not allow full growth then that may not allow a new individual to reach maturity, or the chance for a normal life."

"All human parents contributes to the creation of their new borns, and according to science Tech knowledge, the new individual sex is determined at conception."